WHEN HOPE
BECOMES LIFE

When Hope Becomes Life

A Five-Time Surrogate Mother Shares Her Truth About Surrogacy

Susan A Ring

ALSO BY SUSAN A RING

The Unexpected Mother

FULL CIRCLE PRESS

Full Circle Press books may be purchased for other educational, business, or sales promotional use. For further information, please e-mail us at fullcirclepress01@gmail.com
Full Circle Press
Los Angeles, California

FIRST EDITION

Book Jacket, Pictures, and Page Design: Susan A. Ring, Los Angeles, California.

Library of Congress Cataloging-in-Publication Data is available upon request.

ISBN 978-1-7336266-0-6

For my husband, Paul,
my children, Brian, Steven, Nevaeh,
and all of my surrogate children.

—With love and gratitude

CONTENTS

AUTHOR'S NOTE

This book details my journeys as a surrogate mother along with all the unfathomable and unpredictable challenges and circumstances that occurred as a result of my choices to help intended parents grow their families. I share my story with unflinching honesty. It contains mature scenes.

While my story has been told many times on television, including PBS's Bloodlines, Dr. Oz, and Dr. Phil, with various news stations, and in magazines, including O, The Oprah Magazine (December, 2003), O's Top Ten Anniversary Special (May, 2010), and People Magazine, (March 2016), along with international magazines, none told the entire story.

It's important to note that I was a surrogate mother and gave birth to eight surrogate babies, two singletons and three sets of twins, for five different families throughout an entire decade of my life — all of my forties. Each surrogacy endeavor is called a journey. Each of my five journeys as a surrogate mother was different and unique. Book One, The Unexpected Mother, is about my first two surrogate journeys. Book Two, When Hope Becomes Life, is about my experience with O Magazine's photo shoot and the next three surrogate journeys, and Book Three, Full Circle, details my life after surrogacy, when I was still not able to give up pregnancy even after finding the love I craved, for which the consequences were life-threatening and brought me full circle, and left me infertile.

In writing this book I relied on my notes, personal journals, many paper napkins, consultations with people who appear in the book, and calling up my own memories of these events. I have changed the names of most individuals in this book, and, in some cases, modified identifying details to preserve anonymity. There are no composite characters or events in this book.

Someone I loved once gave me
a box full of darkness.
It took me years to understand
that this too, was a gift.

—Mary Oliver

ONE

A PICTURE IS WORTH A THOUSAND WORDS

September 2003

I was getting my hair and makeup done in the bathroom of the home where the photo shoot for O, The Oprah Magazine was taking place when Ron, the photographer who was hired by Oprah Winfrey's staff said, "I have a really cool prop for our photo shoot."

I nodded to him as one of the hairdressers tugged on my hair to straighten it.

I believed the prop would probably be baby-related due to all of the baby items throughout the house planted close to the top of the hill in Hollywood Hills, California. My story was about my first surrogacy journey and I was told they wanted to use the theme of babies. There was a second stroller by the front door, a high chair near the kitchen, a playpen in the center of the living room, and white cotton diapers thrown to the edges of a few chairs throughout the house. Ron wanted to do the shoot with a crib in the baby's room too. Oprah's producer said they picked this site because the people that lived there just had a baby, and they wanted to use the baby items for the photo shoot.

I was already a little on edge because I had trouble finding the house. The address on the house was impossible to read from the ivy growing over all the houses in the neighborhood. The dirt-paved roads going up the hills were so narrow you had to stop for cars coming down so they could pass. I anxiously wondered what the drive would be like going back down later. I stressed out and wondered if I was in the right area because it was taking so long to find the house. Finally, I saw a little red door with a stroller in front, ivy all over the top of the house, and four cars in the driveway. I re-checked the address and description. This was the house.

Oprah's people mentioned that I could bring my boys, Brian, who was twelve, and Steven, ten, because I was a single mother and the shoot was going to take more than a few hours so they scheduled it after school hours, I had them bring their homework to do at a table nearby while I had a few pictures taken. The boys were talking away on the ride to the house wondering what the photo shoot would be like. I was given a list of dos and don'ts with colors to wear or not wear, and outfits to bring. I asked the producer for O Magazine, Tess, if I could bring our lab-retriever dog, Boomer, so I could create the feel of Oprah's life and her love for dogs to add warmth into her magazine for the story.

Tess said, "No, just yourself and the boys."

I mean, seriously, what did I know about interviews and photo shoots? All I knew was what I read and viewed as a consumer in the magazines. I had no idea what made me think I was prepared and could make recommendations for Hollywood photo shoot!

During the time I was getting my hair and makeup done I had a lot of time to think, and I thought about how crazy that it had been only a few weeks since I got that call at work from Oprah's people asking if I'd like to share my story with Oprah! At first, I thought it was a crank call because I couldn't imagine how anyone could get my work number.

I worked at a highly secure think tank in Los Angeles in the middle of a secure building with no windows, where just about everything was gray metal or painted gray. My desk was temporarily in the middle of a lobby that I shared with an office co-worker. I was staring at the heavy entry firewall doors in front of me with six offices, three on each side of me, when the phone rang on my tiny wood desk, most certainly from the 1960's that I could barely fit my long legs under.

"Susan Ring?"

"Yes, this is Susan," I said brightly. I was on my best behavior because I was a temporary employee trying to make my way to a full-time employee. It was an excellent company to work for and I'd only been there a few months.

"I am a producer for Oprah Winfrey working for O, The Oprah Magazine in Chicago. We saw your PBS special called Bloodlines, and Oprah would like to know if you'd like to share your amazing surrogacy story with O, The Oprah Magazine?"

SILENCE

"Susan?"

"Yes, um… yes." I felt my eyes open big and I knew I had to choose my next words wisely because everyone in the office would be able to hear whatever I would say next. No one at work knew about my surrogacy journeys, and I didn't want to risk my new job by revealing too much while so many people could overhear me.

I remembered thinking, 'Is this a real call? The Oprah Winfrey?'

I told the producer, "Yes, that would be okay."

"What would be okay?" she asked.

"Um, the story." I quieted my voice to almost a whisper, but it didn't work. I'd have to answer with full sentences to have an actual conversation. "Yes, I'd be happy and excited to share my story with O Magazine. Oprah wants my story? Is this real?" I asked hesitating.

After the call, almost everyone was out of their offices standing around my tiny desk asking questions. I spent the next hour explaining my story to my boss and my co-workers. It felt so odd to tell people my story, especially my co-workers. I still felt terribly vulnerable.

The two makeup artists and the hairstylist finally finished with me. The long haired-blonde with huge, thick, black eyelashes said, "Take a quick look-see at yourself, honey, then you can go on in and Ron will take pictures."

I checked my appearance in the mirror and was startled by the heavy makeup painted on my face. It was thick and felt like a Halloween mask. I didn't wear a lot of makeup and wanted to look natural but figured they must know what they are doing. I didn't know anything about how camera lens work with makeup. My hair was straightened so stiff it didn't move at all.

I walked into the dining room where Ron, the photographer was setting up, and then walked further into the living room to check on Brian and Steven. When I looked at the boys, Brian looked directly at me and raised his eyebrows. He elbowed his younger brother who then looked up at me. Steven flatly smiled and rolled his eyes. I smiled hoping I wouldn't look like I felt in the pictures. The makeup was overdone. I felt fake and nothing like myself.

I turned and walked back to look for direction from Ron. His shoulder length, blackish-gray streaked hair moved quickly when he turned his head around fast. He was putting everything in its place while mumbling about the "bad lighting." He seemed anxious, tinkering with his camera, never meeting my eyes.

"I want you to hold this sign in front of you, like near the center of your body, and I'll catch a few shots when you're ready," he said.

He handed me a sign. I looked at the large white letters on a red painted background as he handed it to me, but I couldn't read it because my eyelashes were so thick with mascara they were sticking to the top of my eyelids when I blinked.

With both hands, I put the sign in front of me, and then saw the message: "FOR RENT."

My heart dropped. I felt a thick dread in my throat. I looked at Ron incredulously, but he had no expression and wouldn't look me in the eyes. I swear to God my heart fell onto the floor and shattered into a thousand little pieces. I'm not much of a crier but the tears came rolling down my cheeks at a rapid pace.

The makeup was ruined. My self-worth was flattened. Shame. Doubt. Fear. All were rapidly creeping in. I thought I'd gotten over a lot of those feelings after my first two journeys. I thought I was over it.

Shame is a soul-eating emotion and I felt it wash over my body like a thick coat of muck. Every single bad feeling I could feel about myself, and my past, came bubbling up.

"What?" I said in a broken, shattered defense. "You want me to hold this in front of my body?" It takes a lot to beat me over the head and make me cry, but I have to admit, I was broken instantly. I looked over at my boys and didn't want them to know what just happened but knew it might be impossible to keep it from them. Their books were open and pencils were up so they weren't watching. I looked away so they couldn't see tears streaming down my face. I walked over to the other side of the camera set-up near a corner.

"Well, let's go, Susan, what's wrong?" Ron said when he finally looked at me face to face. He pulled his long hair over his ear with one hand and said, "For Christ's sake, what's wrong?" I noticed the gray streaks in his hair matched his scraggly beard.

"You're serious. Oh my God," I said in an almost whisper. My tears were streaming heavier now. I tried to hold them back, but it wasn't happening, and it was useless with all the makeup on. I looked down at my hands as I tried to stop my tears and saw flat black lines and blotches of color.

"Did I say something wrong?" he asked again.

Was I being overly emotional? I didn't know what to say. It's not every day that a major, international magazine wants you to hold a FOR RENT sign in front of your body.

I put my head down to my chest and looked away from him. I dropped the sign to my side, embarrassed as it slipped onto the floor.

"What, what is the matter? Jesus," he said again. I looked at him a few feet away.

"I'll never use that sign on or near my body," I said. My self-worth was at an all-time low, and I could feel the childhood familiarity of warm shame rushing from the top of my head to the bottom of my toes. Again.

Ron didn't know what surrogacy meant to me. He was a man and would probably understand less than a woman would, but he was human. There was no excuse. He obviously never had infertility problems. I knew for a fact he'd never seen the joyful face of someone who had tried so many times to have a child but had been denied over and over again the moment they've been given the most precious gift in the world, life.

There are so many precious gifts one can give to another but handing over a baby that you've grown in your body with tender loving care to the open arms of their much-awaited parents is unlike anything else I've ever experienced — and is something I will never forget.

It was like that for my own mother, too. She didn't fully understand until she saw the beauty of surrogacy in action at that moment, and what it does for a family — that is when she saw the miracle of how it works.

Surrogacy was the one thing I did for myself. I loved being pregnant and feeling life inside of me, so it was a win-win. To me, it was beautiful in every way, but how could I ever convey this to Ron? Should I even try?

Truthfully, I got angry and was tired of trying to protect surrogacy. It was usually one person at a time, and I said the same things over and over, again and again, and I was exhausted by it.

Was the whole magazine article going to portray my story as a womb for rent despite my efforts? I was very clear and had told staffers at O, The Oprah Magazine, that I did not want my story to be portrayed in a negative, less than fair way. Often, if not always, the media would exploit surrogacy and surrogates as "poor innocent women renting out their bodies," which was not true, and more importantly was not my story and not at all how I wanted my story to be portrayed.

I always felt that being a surrogate mother and helping another woman become a mother was one of the most feminist things I'd ever done. Feminist because as a woman we have a choice with what we do with our bodies. My choice was to understand what it might be like to not be able to have a baby, and then make a decision to act compassionately and help another woman. In turn, when I gave birth for a woman who couldn't not do it herself, there was an amazing and profound sisterhood strength, and it greatly empowered me as a woman.

I thought it would be different with Oprah because she talks about empowering women all the time. I didn't want to be a part of the whole 'womb for rent' idea. The producer confirmed to me before the shoot that it would be nothing of the kind. They were going to tell my story the way it happened, so I couldn't believe Ron could ask me to do such a thing and expect me to be on board. The kind of pictures Ron wanted to take would come back and haunt a person forever.

I reached for the camera around Ron's neck and said, "Here, you take the sign and let me take a few shots of you holding that sign in front of your body. Then tell me how you feel."

"Jesus Fucking Christ, Susan." He looked at me like I was some weird, crazed woman and jerked his camera away from me. "Makeup! Again. for Christ's sake!" he yelled. A few of the makeup artists came in quickly, looked at me, and began to lead me back to the bathroom for more makeup.

Ron yelled, "Fuck! Can we get some wine in here, please? We need to loosen some people the fuck up."

I looked over at the boys to see if they were watching. They weren't because they had turned on the television to watch cartoons. When Ron's voice went up, they looked over our way. Both their faces showed concern. They saw me looking at them, and quickly put their heads down and back into their books.

"Starting with you," I said to Ron. I turned around to go back into makeup. I felt like leaving. The fight or flight feelings were growing stronger in my mind, but I didn't know what to do. I knew if I left they wouldn't call me back again. I wanted to be in O, The Oprah magazine, but at what cost to myself? What was I going to say to the boys? I wanted to share my story but I didn't want it to be about renting my womb. I never rented my womb. Three little words that I couldn't stand about surrogacy, that bothered me so much and made me so angry: Womb. For. Rent.

I thought about my strong feelings of self-worth as a woman, mother, and surrogate mother. My rage then reduced to a low simmer. I decided to move forward and get through the photo shoot without holding the sign in front of my body. I couldn't be sure I was done crying so I tried to gather myself together and just breathe.

Needless to say, the afternoon didn't go like I thought it would. My face was swollen from crying and my eyes were still glazed over even when I got home. Maybe no one would ever really know because they don't know me, but I knew. The shame went deep. The pictures turned out okay, but I couldn't smile for the life of me.

The next day the photo shoot bothered me so much that I called Tess over at O Magazine. I wanted to let her know what happened.

Almost crying, I told her what happened. She seemed sympathetic and her words were reassuring. "We would not tolerate such a thing, we're sorry that happened to you at the photo shoot."

Later, we had a few emails going back and forth, and Tess continued to reassure me that I had nothing to worry about and no one from O, The Oprah Magazine had instructed Ron to use the sign. I felt more relieved, and more confident that my story would be portrayed in a positive way. I felt a little more excited going through the endless phone calls, and emails with questions about my story, the people involved, and all the details. I'd start with one department and then be switched to another department and be asked more legal questions, and then on to the fact-checking department. I worked with several people in that department for close to a month, with at least what seemed like forty or more phone calls going back and forth checking and re-checking my story and every last thing.

In between telling the story to O staffers came the meeting with the freelance writer who was hired by O Magazine to write the story. I offered to pick up the writer, Jessica, at the airport and she took me up on it. She stayed at a hotel nearby, and I took two vacation days off work so we could go over all the details of my story.

Secretly, I wished I were the one writing the article. I'd always wanted to be a writer.

Jessica and I got to work on the interview, the questions were endless and were ones I'd already gone through with O Magazine. Jessica had a short blonde hairstyle cut above the ears and wore comfortable jeans and a t-shirt. As we sat together at my dinner table she made me feel at ease with her warm personality and all the legal papers from the courts, photos, and many personal items spread between us.

We talked about the first set of twins I gave birth to as a surrogate mother. I felt a strong responsibility to protect the twins with their new names, and didn't want Michael or Jackie, the parents who contracted with me to have them (and ultimately gave them up), to think they could come back into their lives if they saw pictures of them, and neither did the twins' new parents. It all felt raw and not healed yet with me, and my protective mode went up each time she asked about their names. I told her I didn't want the twins' names used in the article, and absolutely no to pictures of them.

Jessica seemed like a simple person, like me, and I related to her well. She asked really personal questions, but I felt like I could be an open book with her. I was opening my life to the level I felt comfortable to share.

She asked, "How do you date when you're a surrogate mother?"

I gave her a few situations that I experienced while dating during surrogacy journeys, like the time I told a potential date that I'd be pregnant soon and would it bother him? She laughed because the stories were kind of funny in an ironic sort of way.

She asked about my boys. "How do you pull off being a single mother and being a surrogate mother?"

"I just do it, like any mother would who wants a life of her own with her children."

Often the biggest question I get that is rarely put into print is, "How can you let go of a child you carry for nine months?"

I told Jessica that question was always easy to answer for me: The baby isn't mine to begin with. I prepared myself that the baby is not my baby even before I began.

We were like two girlfriends telling stories by the end of her visit. I trusted her.

I never realized all the time that goes into a story for a magazine. I had asked Tess at O Magazine if I could review the article before publication to get a sneak peek. "No, it's not possible to review any article before publication. All magazines work that way" she said.

I trusted that, but still felt uneasy. I reiterated to Jessica that I did not want the story to have a negative spin, even though, honestly, it was kind of a nightmare.

"I'll tell it just like I see it Susan. It will be factual," Jessica said.

It had been only a few weeks since the photo shoot, so I stayed with the feeling that anything coming straight from Oprah would be fair and truthful. I stayed with that gut feeling: 'Oprah is all empowering. She won't belittle my story,' I thought.

Months later I got word via email from Tess at O, The Oprah Magazine that my story would be in the December 2003 issue of the magazine. A few weeks later when the magazine was out, I hurried over to the local grocery store excited to pick up a copy. When I found it, I glanced at the cover and slipped through the pages one after another looking for headlines to see anything resembling my story.

I went to the index of the magazine and glanced at all of the subtitles to find anything close to my story and didn't see anything. I turned it over to look at the front cover because I remembered that Tess said it would be an exclusive story so it would be on the cover. Then, when I glanced again, there it was on the bottom left in bold, capital red letters.

"WOMB FOR RENT: The Stork Brought Trouble… Divorce, Bankruptcy and the Mother of all Lawsuits."

My heart dropped, this time to the bottom of my being right there in Ralph's supermarket. I was crushed. It ached more deeply when I remembered it was an international publication. I hadn't even read the story yet, and I was paralyzed. I then looked around me thinking that every person in that store was watching, judging me.

The three words I hated most about surrogacy were on the front cover of an international magazine, with my story, my face representing a 'womb for rent.'

Then I looked at the article. I read a response from the woman for whom I carried the twins in my second surrogacy journey: Jackie, the mother, had talked to Jessica about the story. All she had to say about me was, "I feel she is a kidnapper." This nearly knocked me over. Jackie was the one who never showed up at the hospital to pick up her babies — and said she didn't want them. Dear God, I thought, the drama just keeps going. Then, I wondered, what exactly did I expect? Worst of all, there was a picture of me with my boys. Had I known they were going to use it I would never have agreed to have my children photographed that day.

The story was actually factual and spot on and yet... O, The Oprah Magazine, while keeping their word that "Womb For Rent" wouldn't be in the story, put those words on the fucking cover. I couldn't get my mind off it. It was a label of complete demoralization and utter embarrassment.

I was stunned. How could such a demeaning a title be used after I honestly shared one of the most vulnerable times in my life, after explaining that surrogacy is not at all "renting a womb," and after giving birth to three real live human beings (at that point) for another family. I experienced a deep visceral feeling of being stripped and naked, then my mind went to feeling like a shivering 'womb for rent,' a commodity, a rental — less than human.

Then, another jab in the table of contents of the magazine just after Jessica's name: the story was listed as, "a court womb drama." I'm sure a few people got a great laugh out of that one. I cried like a freaking baby. I stuffed the humiliation down deeper until I couldn't feel or find it.

I looked at what surrounded my story in the magazine, the other articles. My story took up quite a bit of space, four pages. The biggest celebrity story was Oprah visiting Julia Roberts at her ranch, and they were "bringing on the margaritas." I thought, 'right now I could use a fucking margarita, a very strong one!'

Everything seemed awe-inspiring in the December issue of O, The Oprah Magazine, except my story.

I was not the story you made of me, Oprah.

I couldn't let it go, it plagued my thoughts night and day. I heard from every friend and acquaintance I ever knew, those who knew about my story and those who did not. I got a lot of emails from people I didn't know who wrote some very mean things.

I wanted to know who made the choice for "Womb For Rent." Why did that have to be on the cover? I sent an angry letter to Oprah after sitting on it for three days, asking why, and titled it, Things I know For Sure. I was angry, and at the top I wrote, "#1- Even the most respected woman in the world can't be trusted." I'm not proud of the letter I sent to Oprah now, but I was so angry then. It felt good to write it. I ended up sending it when it was really meant to just get out my feelings. It was on a night when I was at my lowest that I sent the letter to Oprah Winfrey.

I wondered, though, how was I going to protect myself from the media and everyone I knew if I was still so damn temperamental about three little words?

"Womb. For. Rent."

Why did it bother me so much? The reason blared into my face like the bright sun with reality: because it came from Oprah Winfrey, a billionaire media icon, the woman who was on top of a very short list of people I looked up to for years. And that wasn't even 'a short list.' In fact, Oprah was the only one on it.

Oprah was the one who helped me through my own childhood trauma issues, as she's helped so many women. She was the first one who said on national television to the world of child abuse survivors "It is not your fault."

That statement she made opened up my own healing of childhood abuse. It brought a lot of childhood pain up and out of my body. I started to deal with my issues, and it helped me deal with the shame I had buried so long ago as a little girl. She helped me grow in ways I was never able to thank her for. It just didn't make sense. Why would she do such a thing? I felt the deep trust I had in her turn into deep betrayal.

I started to berate myself for letting it happen. I relived the photo shoot over and over again. A lot of my friends and family, if not all, told me I was overreacting, that the article was more in my favor, it told the truth of my story. But I just couldn't get over those three little words on the cover and in the table of contents.

I wondered how I got myself into this kind of high drama situation again, not thinking that maybe it's because it is a highly controversial subject. Many didn't believe in it, many did. Maybe Oprah was one that didn't think highly of surrogacy? For a lot of people, surrogacy was black and white, you either were positive about it or you hated it. No gray. No in-between. If this was the case, I just wish I had known beforehand — in which case I would not have done it.

Adding to my suspicions, O, The Oprah Magazine published a scathing article about reproductive choices the month after my article came out. I was truly shocked.

I needed answers and began calling every phone number I had of the contacts at O Magazine. I even called her two personal assistants one last time, who said to me, "Only one person does Oprah's covers, and that is Oprah herself."

I never heard back from Oprah, herself, but a week or two after that I made my last daily angry call going nowhere, I received a gorgeous clear glass bowl of beautiful cut white roses with a note that read, "From the Staff At O, The Oprah Magazine."

TWO

INDECISIONS

I met Madeline (Maddie for short) and Ben a few months before the Oprah article came out in December of 2003. They had somehow learned about the story through someone who knew someone in the infertility world, and hunted down the agency owned by Lauren and Tracey, the two women I worked with for my first two surrogacy journeys.

Lauren called me and said, "I have two people, Ben and Madeline, prospective intended parents, that really want to meet you."

Lauren, Tracey, and I still had a 'friendly' relationship, but it had been strained with all that happened in our first two journeys. We managed to stay in touch but our relationship that dipped into the personal always turned out to be just a business relationship.

I was at a point where I was settling down with a great job and wasn't sure I wanted to do surrogacy again- I was still trying to make up my mind whether I wanted to go through with the whole surrogacy journey again. It was a huge undertaking and took a lot more energy after each journey. I knew what to look out for this time, though, and I knew any journey forward would not be like the last two.

I was unsure about working with Lauren and Tracey again because I didn't need the hand-holding they provided as an agency. Really, all the agency did was make the match then hold your hand through the process. I felt their fee came at a high price for hand-holding which included making appointments for me, but I could do that myself. I thought about doing it independently by myself because I knew the process and what needed to be done. I would use a legal contract and manage all the details. I thought I would be better going at it alone, without the agency.

The only drawback to that was it would be hard to find people who needed a surrogate without an agency because I could not advertise my services just anywhere. The agency also attended appointments with a surrogate, but I certainly didn't need anyone coming with me to them, except the parents if they chose to. The agency also called every other week to see how I was doing. That's it. Maybe I was just a very independent person and saw no need for their service, except for the matchmaking part.

But Maddie and Ben had gone to them to learn about me, so I felt obligated to meet them, and, if I chose to work with them I would have to go through Lauren and Tracey.

I was still in a funk after the second surrogacy. Giving up the twins for adoption was harder than I thought it would be, and it took me quite a bit of time to adjust after the adoption was final, for my life to settle down.

Deep down, I desperately wanted to have a good surrogacy experience. I didn't share this thought with just anyone, but I really wanted to see what it would be like to do a surrogacy for someone who really wanted a family. I was curious to see if I would have any connection with Maddie and Ben.

I started to see that the matching process of people was probably if not the most important part of a surrogacy journey. It was like the match process for someone you meet online or someone you meet in person, hoping for a good relationship. It's real connections that make or break a relationship. It's people of like mind that get along together well.

I decided to meet them and called Lauren back to arrange an appointment for us to get together, and kept it to myself.

We met on an early spring day at the agency with Tracey and Lauren. I sensed right away that Ben was a gentle kind of man. He was handsome, tall, with spots of gray in his brownish hair. His smile was warm. Maddie had a very soft, intelligent way about herself. She was tall, too, and her blonde hair just barely touched her shoulders and her dark blue eyes complemented her warm face. They both kept their tall bodies fit, and I could tell they took care of themselves.

As we introduced ourselves and got to know one another, Maddie told me she was a volunteer for several non-profit organizations involving art and books. Ben owned his own successful electrical company.

I sat on a couch and Ben and Maddie sat in chairs across from me. Lauren and Tracey stayed for ten or fifteen minutes as we chatted then left the room. Ben asked if I wanted to see a few pictures of their family. There were three photo albums spread out on the table. He grabbed one and handed it to me, and he joined me on the couch. I opened the first page.

He pointed to a picture and his face lit up. "This picture is of Maddie's brothers' kids, the four there, all girls."

I looked at the pictures of people I didn't know at family events like weddings and parties, but it was enjoyable because I felt like Maddie and Ben were inviting me to be a part of their family by sharing.

"That one is Alec, he's a character," Maddie said softly laughing and joining me on the other side of the couch. She paused for a moment in reflection like you do with photographs that mean something to you. She smiled and pointed, "He was going to get the other kids," she said as she laughed.

The picture was of a little boy who was maybe three years old, holding a garden hose and wanting to spray the other dressed up kids. He wore the biggest grin, and being a mom of boys, I could understand that he probably was quite a handful. We slowly took a walk down memory lane as I was getting to know their family. They talked a lot about their family, and I told them about my boys, Brian and Steven, and a little about my brothers and sisters.

There were way too many children to count in the pictures and trying to keep them straight with names was impossible. They were all cute little kids, fourteen and under, that all looked the similar, with blonde hair, light brown hair and green or blue eyes galore. They were adorable.

We had been on the couch sharing their family photo albums for close to an hour when Maddie said, "We've been trying for almost fifteen years, and had numerous negative cycles with the best of the best, Cornell, Stanford, and a few other notable centers, and we have nothing to show for it." Her voice sounded so sad, lost. "Just this month the doctors told us to start thinking about getting a surrogate mother. That's when we heard about your story through friends and it felt like we needed to meet you."

I smiled thinking that I was happy to meet them both.

Ben said, "It's been so hard because with all the negative cycles we've been through, at least what, fourteen, fifteen cycles, and not one doctor can tell us what is wrong." His voice cracked with emotion when he said, "They call it 'unexplained infertility.'"

I was perplexed and wondered why the best doctors specializing in infertility couldn't figure out why Maddie and Ben couldn't conceive. It had to be something, I thought.

I was truly impressed they were still married after all these years, after all the heartache they've been through together. It takes a lot to go through so many negative cycles, with so much disappointment, and still stay reasonably close. They seemed to be such a nice couple, in an authentic way. Real.

Ben looked over at Maddie and smiled lovingly at her.

Their relationship reminded me of my older brother's marriage. Harold and his wife, Katrina, had been married twenty-plus years, and it was the only relationship I'd ever looked up to all of my life, the only one I had any sense of what a good, loving relationship looked like, a solid, supportive and compassionate love.

Ben handed me a picture and said, "This is my nephew. I'm one of two kids, just my sister and me. I'm the only one without children. Maddie is one of five, and the only one without children. We'd be happy with just one child."

I was touched, already on board, but didn't want to agree until I had time to think a bit more and digest everything about doing another surrogacy.

There was no doubt that I hungered to feel a baby move inside me one more time. I loved the gentle and firm kicks deep within my body. The nudges of life reminded me I was growing a miracle. It energized me in a way that is hard to explain. It felt like the hormones engaged every part of my body and lubricated my joints. I got excited when I thought about birthing life, and that quick high hit knowing I'd be that way for nine whole months. I remembered the moments, the twinges, when it felt like life grabbed onto the tissue of my uterus like a hungry organism implanting itself to make a home and grow inside my body. Sometimes, I was absolutely certain I could feel it take hold.

I wondered if other women felt the way I did. Why did I need this, or at the very least, why did I feel a need to do it again? I thought about it for about five minutes and then realized I didn't care about my motivations because it was easier to do what I wanted and what felt good to me. 'And why not do something you're really good at, right?' I thought to myself.

Part of this was convincing myself to do it again. But maybe, it was because deep down there may have been a part of me that said I shouldn't do it. I chose to ignore those feelings. Denial works great that way. Later, I'd face the real questions of why.

Lauren came back into the room and asked, "Tracey left for home, but I thought I'd join you all to see how it's going?" It was the end of a long day and she seemed eager to leave. Maddie said, "Oh my gosh Lauren, we were talking so much I didn't realize how much time had gone by!"

We promised to meet again soon.

I'd find out later that Lauren, Tracey, and I we were never friends at all. They were instructed by legal counsel to "keep me close" until the legal statutes went by. I'm sure there were legal reasons for them, and they didn't want to get sued, but I really thought we were friends, not best of friends, but friends, nonetheless.

It did cross my mind to sue them for all of the emotional distress they caused but I decided not to because they helped me take care of my own kids during the journeys. My oldest son, Brian, was in Lauren's daughter's grade and class. They had been friends since elementary school. I really should have known better than to think we were friends because their lifestyle did not match ours, and we did not share any friends or really do anything personal together.

After the proper amount of time went by for me to have any legal retribution, Lauren, Tracey, and I wouldn't speak again. A few years later, they would end up having a major personal disagreement between themselves and stopped being best friends. They never talked about it to anyone outside their own circle. I heard this through the gossip lines in our infertility groups. I ran into Lauren once around town, and we made small talk for maybe one minute. She told me they ended up selling their egg donation and surrogacy business to a woman who worked in their office who then wound up being wanted by the FBI for "selling babies." This all took years to happen, but in the end, this is what happened to their agency.

I had put off my last postpartum visit after the twins, and realized I'd better get into my OB/GYN doctor if I was going to ask for his authorization to do another surrogacy. Spring was in full force with flowers blooming everywhere. It was my favorite time of year. I started feeling happy again and had something to look forward to, another surrogacy. It seemed to fulfill my life, and I couldn't wait to help Maddie and Ben have a family and learn why they couldn't have children.

Dr. Kazman's office was your typical OB/GYN office in Los Angeles with pictures of thousands of babies all over the hallway walls. He was a doctor to many in town, along with many celebrities. On my last visit he told me that he delivered Shaquille O'Neal's, the NBA star basketball player's baby close to when I gave birth to the twins. He was telling me how O'Neal is over seven-foot something tall and barely fit through the doorway so he had to duck to go through the door to see his children be born. I didn't care much for celebrities, but I knew who Shaq was because of my boys. They loved sports and knew all the names of the players in all sports. (Both Brian and Steven had a deep passion for baseball and would love to play professionally.) They would have loved this story. Dr. Kazman was a popular and busy doctor in the community.

I was interested in getting some feedback from him so I could understand my own passion with surrogacy. It was something I thought of as an obsession but maybe it was hedging toward addiction.

"Dr. Kazman, what is the definition of addiction in the medical world?" I wasn't worried about it, but I was curious.

"When 'want' becomes 'need,' that is what defines an addiction." He said without missing a beat.

"Are you talking about surrogacy?" he asked seriously. His inquisitive steel-gray eyes shone through his round, black-rimmed glasses. He looked straight at me as he was about to listen to my heart with his stethoscope. He had a boyish, cute look about him, the way his bangs fell softly over his glasses. I always thought of him like a big brother.

"Yeah," I said quietly.

"Well, you might think of other ways to have a job and get paid." He put his head down to write on my chart. I wondered what he wrote.

"I have an everyday job," I said. I felt very put off that that he assumed I was doing it for the money. I added, "And, I love being pregnant, Dr. Kazman. I thought you knew that about me. I don't do it for the money."

"You're probably the best surrogate mother I know, Susan. Just take it easy with your body, it's the only one you've got."

I could tell he saw what he said hurt my feelings. Dr. Kazman wouldn't be who he was if he didn't speak his mind, and I respected him for that, but he seemed especially pissed off today.

"If you're addicted to anything, Susan, it'd be to the hormones of pregnancy, not the pregnancy itself."

I wondered how he would know because he'd never been pregnant. Maybe he was right though, because it sounded about right. I did love the hormones when I started the cycling protocol for surrogacy before the transfers of embryos. The hormones were prescribed at a higher than normal dosage so my body could prepare for pregnancy. Then I remembered that maybe he was a little put off with me from several months back when I didn't choose his friends, the movie producer and his attorney wife, as parents for the twins. Maybe that was it. 'Probably,' I thought.

I didn't ask him for approval to be a surrogate this time around because I thought maybe I wouldn't need it, being that I'd never had a C-section and all my pregnancies were healthy, and normal. Everything about this visit felt terrible and made me feel uneasy. I wasn't sure I wanted to see him again as a doctor. This was the first time we clashed like this.

I thought about his answer about addiction for a long time after I left his office. I let it sink in. I didn't think I needed to be pregnant, but I knew I wanted to be pregnant.

In my eyes, there was no amount of money you could put on a human life, and believe me, I don't know any surrogates who made a lot of money being surrogates. I saw the surrogacy deal more as a win-win for both sides. The compelling part of it was that the win for the couple would be they would be able to experience being parents and have a family. The win of it for me was going through the process happily to make the parents' dreams come true, and have a little bit of extra cash to help my kids with college. What I really wanted and dreamed about was having a home for the boys. A real home to call our own is what would make my dreams come true.

I came to the conclusion there was seriously no way I would ever make enough as a single mother to buy a house in our area with my job, surrogacy, and even a second and third job. It was going to be impossible.

So I made our home anywhere we were all together.

THREE

SURROGACY IN THE REAL WORLD

few months after the twins were adopted in February of 2002, Terrie and I received word that we would have to move again. We weren't happy with the notice but there was nothing we could do. Our landlord explained that he wanted to move back into the house with his wife and two small children so they could attend the school across the street. I knew this would happen the day he told us his wife was expecting. We were devastated that we had to move. We loved that little house.

Terrie and I had been friends since our elementary school years, and roommates, years before when we went to college together. We had been living together again after my divorce when we both needed roommates to make ends meet.

We lived in a little beach town next to the ocean where rents had spiked up every single year, and it was getting harder to find a house I could afford. I wanted to keep the boys in a house instead of an apartment because it was important to me for them that they have a house with lawn where they could play and run around with Boomer, our dog, and it seemed to be real that my options were getting slimmer and slimmer, especially finding a home accepting dogs.

Just as important was location. I wanted a house where the boys could go to the same schools and one that was close to my job.

I loved my job, as much as you can love working for someone else and checking in with someone every day, Monday through Friday, 8am to 5pm. But I really did enjoy going to work and I liked the people I worked with.

Well, most of the people. There are always those few that spoil the feeling of being happy at work. There was one person who hated me that I worked in human resources. Her name was Carol. She worked on the other side of the same floor as me and made it clear to anyone who would listen how much she hated me. Co-workers would confidentially tell me what she said, and apparently she hated me because I was a surrogate mother. Although people told me what she was saying, I still found it hard to believe that she felt so strongly about me. I decided to test it and see if what they were saying was true.

One day as we passed each other while walking in opposite directions in the dimly lit hallway at work where conversations often happened among co-workers, I looked directly at her and said, "Hi Carol, how are you today?" She didn't even look up at me. She kept her head down and went along her way as if I weren't there at all. As she passed me, I stopped and watched her walk away from me.

'Whoa, it's true,' I silently said to myself after she passed me. Man, if silence could talk. I could feel her anger, the bad energy vibes, all thick and closed off.

Carol wasn't the only person at work who disliked me because I was a surrogate mother. Word had spread pretty quickly around the corporation after the Oprah article came out, and I was judged from the right and the left and came to have enemies without ever knowing any of them personally.

Some people from different departments would stop me and say to my face, "Are you that surrogate lady? There should be no such thing as surrogacy. There are too many un-adopted kids in the world." They said these things with deep emotion, sometimes happy, oftentimes sad, or just plain angry. They'd wait for me to reply. I would usually say I was in a hurry picking up something from another department and duck out as soon as I could.

I loved the ones who would warmly say, "It's the most beautiful thing to do for another person." That's how I felt, and I always hoped a woman would have done it for me if I'd needed help.

Even though not everyone on our campus knew about me (there were thousands of employees) I had a strong feeling that I would need to keep things to myself, keep myself small, and not make waves. I liked my job and I wanted to keep it.

I was an assistant to Kevin, who had been an engineer in another department and decided to take the job as a director in the most unpopular job and department in the company, human resources. Kevin was a few years older than me, very tall, maybe 6'4". I was surprised when he told me he played in a band when he was younger, and that he still played for fun at home.

"It helps my right brain since I do so much left-brain work during the day," he often said. He was such a great boss, easy to talk to, and someone I respected.

The woman who semi-trained me, Alicia worked in human resources as an assistant business manager.

She said she tried at one point to help Kevin, but he had many requests and eventually it made Alicia crazy. She explained it like this: "I hated this position (referring to the position I'd just started working in). There was way too much to do. It caused me a minor emotional breakdown, so I went back to my other job." I listened attentively so I could learn from someone who had been in this position. "Just know, Susan, this job is incredibly stressful because you have to be super organized, and always know every-thing. But don't worry, just do your best," she added as she patted my shoulder.

I loved organization and figured it couldn't be that bad. Alicia also used words to describe Kevin more in a friendly way such as, "an absent-minded professor," which would prove true to an extent because he always had so much on his mind and was incredibly smart. Part of my job would be to remind him of things often, and I did my job with the organization as required.

It was a very highly educated and highly trained company, with more than half of the company holding their PhDs. I was still working in a full-time temporary status, and hoped I'd prove myself enough that I would become full-time permanent soon. They paid for education for employees once they were with the company a certain amount of time, and so it was a potential opportunity for me to go back to school and finish my degree. The company favored those with degrees. It was just a matter of fact for a highly educated think tank in the middle of Los Angeles.

Kevin hired me to help him revamp the performance review process for the company. It'd be just the two of us. Kevin would head up training approximately 300 managers and I would assist him. Others in human resources explained to me that the subject of performance reviews was a very unpopular topic. No one wanted change, especially when reviews might reflect changes in people had to make in their performance. They wanted it to stay just the way it was. Not one person at the company signed up for the job before me. They hired me from the outside. I didn't care how unpopular it was because I'd mop the floors if I had to. I was grateful for this job. It provided excellent benefits for me, and my boys, and it put food on the table.

As I went about my work and requested things for our department, people who had been with the company a long time (there was very little turnover) would ask what department I was in. Some would roll their eyes when I told them and say, "God, I can't wait till that review form change fizzles out. What was management thinking?"

Apparently, I learned quickly, that revamping the current performance review system at the company was a pet project for a certain vice president for some time, but even after a ten-year period it never evolved into a viable, working process.

So, I kept on the outskirts of gossip as much as I could and kept to myself, especially as I was thinking of starting another surrogacy.

Until, there was John. He worked in another building as a highly respected rocket scientist and he visited our bay quite often. Kevin and I had moved into another building with human resources. Our bay (working area) was quite small, but it was just the two of us. It was in an open lobby area and my desk just fit. I graduated from the tiny 1960s wooden desk to a much nicer, bigger one so I could finally fit my legs under it.

John would frequently come by, and always asked a lot of questions about my position and what it was we were trying to do with the new project. Kevin's office and door were directly behind me.

"Why are you changing it?" John would ask. I'd answer his questions as best I could and then eventually refer him to Kevin if I didn't know specifics about his questions.

On occasion, Kevin would overhear John and he'd walk into the bay from his office to answer John's questions when he heard me struggling to explain how we measure performance. I was barely getting updated on new computer software and it would probably take some time before I became an expert in performance review systems. I was always worried I wouldn't have the right answer but at the same time wondered why John was coming over so often.

Then it got a little weird. John kept popping up in my life at work right before lunchtime and away from work. All of a sudden, I was bumping into him several times at the grocery store, or at the mall when I was with the boys. It was so strange and took me by surprise. It seemed odd that I kept bumping into him. After the fifth time, I started to wonder seriously if he was following me, stalking me.

He called me one quiet afternoon at work, and he sounded funny, like nervous, almost like he wanted to say something but didn't. I said, "Can I help you with something?" and cleared my throat. "I keep seeing you everywhere," I said.

Kevin wasn't in his office so I felt free to ask openly.

"Would you like to go out?" He hesitated then said, "Like on a date?"

"Um, sure, okay," I said. I didn't care to mix relationships with work and wondered if it would be okay if I did.

That day after I told John I would go out with him I spoke to a co-worker in another department who had been there for twenty-some years. I asked her what the rules were about people dating in the same company. She said, "Oh yeah, there are many people who date and some who are married in the company, they just don't work in the same department." That seemed okay to me.

John was old school and insisted on picking me up at my house. I was used to meeting dates at restaurants because I didn't feel comfortable bringing them to my home until I knew them. But since we worked together I didn't think about it again. He was handsome, standing about the same height as me. He was maybe just a little bit taller than my 5'10" frame. The boys met him and giggled in the background as I got ready to go out the door. They were not used to seeing me go out on dates but were old enough now to be on their own for a few hours.

Our date was on a Saturday, late afternoon, and John chose a nice Italian restaurant on a popular street not far from the company. When he opened the car door for me, I noticed he smelled so good. The restaurant was swanky and oh-so-Italian. They had the best garlic bread and fancy oils to dip it in. I'd been there one time before on another date that didn't work out. It felt good to be all dressed up again and to get out like a real live grown up, enjoying good company with a nice glass of wine.

I hadn't been on an official date in quite a long time. It'd been almost a year since I broke things off with Adam, my on-again, off-again lover, and I meant it. He wasn't good for me and I needed to stay far away from him.

John had the same brownish/blonde hair as mine and had a short cut that flattered his eyes of green. His smile was warm and inviting. There was something sweetly boyish about him. I couldn't stop thinking about kissing him and stared at his lips off and on as he talked. We hit it off and talked and talked about ourselves for a few hours.

We lived in the same city, and we had many things in common including a love of the beach. He told me he had never been married and had no children. I became curious and wondered why. We'd see each other often in the gym at work. I never cared what I looked like because I was there to work out, and so was he.

He seemed very shy but then said, "I jump from airplanes in search and rescue missions while away from work or sometimes on weekends."

I was impressed and intrigued, and was usually up for trying anything once myself. "Oh, I'd love to do that someday," I said.

He looked a little surprised and said, "I do secure missions, me and the guys."

I nodded like I understood, smiled, and then lifted my glass for a big gulp of wine. I was nervous thinking I couldn't match up to a Ph.D. rocket scientist as a boyfriend. How would he handle me? Could he handle me? Was I being too much? I was always being "too much." What would we look like together? He was definitely an introvert, and I was an extrovert. I was the curious type so I was willing to see what might happen. I hoped he'd kiss me that night, but he didn't, and despite my questions about how we might be, you never know until you get to know someone how it's really going to go. It did go well enough that he asked me out again.

Before my second date with John, Brian and Steven were asking questions about the guy I was dating at work. We'd only had one date, but I often shared my dating life with them, with limits, of course. Brian was in eighth grade, Steven in sixth, so they could understand that Mom had new relationships.

My oldest, Brian, who is fourteen asked, "Did you tell him about being a surrogate mother yet?"

"No, but I'm not sure it's that important to tell him right now" I replied. "I mean that's something I want to do, and I don't need the buy in of a guy I don't even know yet."

As I said it, I realized it was probably a little strong of a reaction to Brian's question, which made me think that maybe Brian had a point. It did matter. If John and I were going to continue to see each other, it would probably be important for him to know my future plans. I told Brian that I'd tell John on the next date.

There was a reason I didn't share it with John yet. Many other dates I've had in the past were not so agreeable to surrogacy. If I mentioned any plans I had for surrogacy or even that I was a surrogate mother our dates would always cut off abruptly. In some ways I was glad because it has to be for the best because we didn't see things the same way. They likely weren't for me and it was best I found out sooner than later.

Visions of myself pregnant with a baby that wasn't John's, raced through my mind. Possible awkward sexual thoughts in a new relationship popped into my head. He wasn't particularly warm in that sweet human way, but maybe I just didn't know him well enough yet.

On our second date, I met John after work for a quick bite. I learned he had no siblings and one aunt. Although he said he didn't like to talk about his family, he shared with me that he was in the middle of a feud with his mother. I talked openly about my family all the time, the one I made with the boys and my friends, and the one I was born into.

"Yes, family connections are often difficult to deal with sometimes," I said putting down my fork so I could talk.

"Speaking of family..." I said, leading into surrogacy while taking another sip of wine, "I've been a surrogate mother in the past."

"Oh... like having a baby for someone else?" he asked as he dabbed his mouth, put his napkin down and put his hands into his lap. Apparently no one at work had told him about me.

"Yes. Exactly." I said matter of factly.

"So, for one couple that was having fertility problems?" he asked.

"Yes, well, it was one couple that I was a surrogate for two times." I immediately saw the possibility that this conversation was going to veer into the drama of my last journey, and I was hesitant to discuss the details of it before I knew if he really understood surrogacy, so I decided to tread lightly.

"Wow, okay, so that's great" he said, still looking shocked with his hands in his lap.

I smiled and nodded. But then he didn't say anything else.

So, okay, it seemed it was a conversation killer in this case, but after John returned from a restroom break he asked me what the journey of a surrogate mother looked like. I felt a little lighter about the conversation then and was happy to indulge his curiosity. However, I suddenly realized that although I had two surrogate journeys, only one was close to normal. I told him about that one, and then he asked about the second one. I told him the story, but not everything.

"My second journey went very wrong. The same couple that I had a little boy for asked me to do it again for them. So, I did. Turns out they ultimately did not want a bigger family and their relationship took a dive. They divorced, then breached our contract when they decided they didn't want more kids after I was already pregnant with their twins. They told me they didn't want their babies, the babies I was pregnant with."

He just stared at me.

Oh shit, there was no other way around it but to explain further.

"I know it's all a lot to digest, John, but it happened, and it's really quite rare. Most surrogate journeys don't go this way. They usually turn out very well."

I took a breath and added, "It's really an amazing thing to do," and picked up my wine glass again.

He looked at me like he was figuring out a puzzle, wondering what he was going to say. 'Anything, God, just say anything.' I wish I could include a picture of his face. The look on it really was priceless.

"It really doesn't happen a lot at all, in fact, my case is the only one I'm aware."

John was polite and asked a few more questions, and I answered them as best I could. I knew we were doomed when he started looking around the restaurant like he needed to think of a reason to leave. We were at the end of our meal, so I handed him his out.

"I signed a contract with another couple to be a surrogate mother again. I'm starting a new journey in two weeks."

He appeared stunned.

I went ahead and finished my wine.

I didn't hear from him or bump into him anywhere mysteriously again outside of work after that second date. A little over a year later, I literally bumped into John in the lunch line at the company cafeteria. Well, I didn't, my twin belly did. He had the same face that he had when I told him I was going to do a surrogacy again. No words, just the surprised look. Okay, maybe this time he raised his eyebrows at the size of my belly, but a lot of people did that all the time.

"Hi John!" I said. He raised his hand a bit to indicate a hello, and then grabbed his tray and put his lunch on it and turned around slowly, then moved on swiftly.

I suddenly felt my skin toughen up, but shame was still there, deep down. It almost felt like my skin was protecting the shame. I cringed.

I began to tell myself that participating in the article for O, The Oprah Magazine might have been a mistake. I felt like I had to hide far, far away from others, and I didn't want to share that I was a surrogate mother. I wanted to hide from everything.

I held out hope that there would be that one guy who would understand, and love me just the way I was, pregnant or not.

Even after the article came out and after the shock of what I was labeled, I always had colorful visions of spreading the good word about surrogacy. It was my passion, and yet it wasn't something people understood or openly accepted. I was okay with that and I'd do my best to help others understand.

I wasn't able to do much good with the O Magazine article, but many friends and family often told me that even bad publicity is good publicity, because surrogacy was getting noticed. That was true, but it seemed like it had a long way to go from the backdoor to the front door.

It took time for me to come around and date again. Sweet time was the only thing that helped.

FOUR

JOURNEY #3 START

Months later, in March 2003, I began my journey with Ben and Maddie. I was excited to start, and they seemed to be, too.

We were working with the best clinic in the mid-Wilshire district of Los Angeles, California. Their success rates for pregnancy outcome were high, and they were so popular people flew in from many different countries to work with them. They were busy.

I'd never worked with them before and I found the drive into Los Angeles from the south bay, under ten miles, would become a problem on certain days and times. Once I found a way around the traffic, my got my schedule to work. I'd start my day at 5:30a.m. to get to the clinic before heading to my job.

On my first visit I went through the same extended medical exam that I did with my first two surrogacy journeys, including the blood work panels for disease. Since I had no medical or pregnancy issues with the previous pregnancies and I was working with the same agency, they didn't require a letter of approval from Dr. Kazman, my OBGYN. We were basically starting over because this was a new doctor and a new clinic with different standards for their protocols.

Around the same time, we were finalizing contracts, finishing psychological clearances, for both parties this time, compared to previous journeys, and getting to know each other better.

For the first time, the journey felt right for me. This couple, Ben and Maddie, made me feel like we were working toward the same goals. We were working together to co-create a family through surrogacy.

They made a few special visits from the Bible Belt of Indiana just to meet my boys. We went out to dinner a few times and had pizza. They got to see how much both boys loved baseball. They talked about the conservative place they lived and made it clear that although they lived in a very religious area they were not religious. Because of more liberal views and abundant agencies, California continually drew people from around the country who wanted to do surrogacy.

It took a few more months to get clearance for our journey from all ends, and as soon as we did, we were ready to move along.

The first reproductive endocrinologist I met with was Dr. Matthews. Before Dr. Matthews came in the room, I was talking with one of the nurses about being single versus being married as a surrogate mother. I told her I was single.

"I see that in the chart," she said, getting all the medical tools ready for the exam. "Good for you, it's not easy doing it all yourself. Dr. Matthews was just recently divorced, too," she said as a matter of fact. It perked me up because it seemed all I was ever meeting were married men.

Dr. Matthews walked in and said, "Hello there." Not only was he recently divorced but he was incredibly handsome, and about my age. I was sitting on the exam table in a gown completely naked underneath, and noticed he had a medium build and had longer hair than most doctors. His long, brownish hair with slight streaks of gray had a slight curl and fell just right at his shoulder.

I felt instant chemistry and was totally surprised when the nurse left the room. His voice was soft during my exam in the next ten minutes or so, and he was completely professional until he walked over to the right side of my body and slid his finger slowly from the top of my rib cage down my leg to my ankle under my gown. It was one complete light touch stroke. It surprised the hell out of me.

My body shuddered from head to toe and it brought me to full attention. I wasn't sure what was going on. He didn't do anything after that, and just smiled. His smile was warm, inviting, and sexy. Was it a come on? Was it flirting? What the heck did he mean by that? It was hot. He was hot.

He was still explaining the protocol, but I wasn't listening to a word he was saying. In my mind, I still felt his finger dance lightly, ticking me down my leg, and thought,

'Oh my, could that be a come on?' I hoped so, but felt frozen to say or do anything.

I brought myself out of my own little fantasy-shocked world when I heard him say, "So do you have the list of things from the nurse you need to do before the transfer?"

What transfer? When and where? Did I get what I needed? "Um, no. No, I didn't," I said, still wondering what just happened.

Dr. Matthews. Whew. I never had an encounter quite like that one with a doctor, and the sexual fantasy side of my mind wouldn't stop. I kept feeling his touch on my body day and night, and could still feel it to this day. His finger took a walk, gliding down my body to my ankle, and I still felt it ten years later! I wondered if we'd have any chance of dating. Then I laughed. He was a renowned, reproductive endocrinologist, and I was a single surrogate mother. Shit.

My chances didn't look good but why did I have to put myself down? Dammit. Well, I still held out huge reserves of hope and I had an unbelievable, creative fantasy-filled mind. Secretly, I wanted to date him in reality and kept wondering if it would ever happen. I couldn't wait to see him again at our next visit.

Okay, then I did what any other woman might do. I told my girlfriend Terrie and we shared quite a few laughs about it. I asked her if any doctor had ever done something like that to her. She said, "Um, no, Susan. No."

"Do you think it was a come on?"

"I don't know. It's odd, that's for sure," she said.

I wasn't done thinking about it and thought about telling Lauren and Tracey. Sometimes we had a girly, girl-friend relationship and talked about hot guys, dating, and men. Even though they were both married and I wasn't, we talked openly about things like that. I know they were my surrogacy agency, but they were personable, sometimes. I wondered if I should tell them about it, and better, wondered if they knew Dr. Matthews. They usually talked about other clinics and seemed to all know each other in the medical field. I wanted to see what chance, if any, I might have with Dr. Matthews.

I was on the phone finalizing appointments with Lauren and decided to indulge her with what happened.

"Wow, Dr. Matthews is hot," I said.

"What'd he do?" Lauren asked curiously.

"Damn, what didn't he do?" I told her everything, and then heard nothing but silence. I knew it was the wrong thing to do. She was in agency mode and not girlfriend mode. It was a mistake to tell her. Dammit. I'm pretty sure she believed me, and knew me well enough to know I wouldn't make this kind of story up.

In reality I knew it was wishful thinking because he was my doctor. Professionally, I knew it was a big no-no. I probably wanted it to be a yes-yes, but it was a professional no-no.

I got a call from the infertility office before my next visit saying I had been switched to another doctor in the group. A well-known, highly respected doctor who also happened to be gay, it turned out, Dr. Wrangler. (I didn't learn he was gay until a little while later from gossip around the infertility office when I had to wait for meds, schedules, or wait in the office for my appointments.) I bet Lauren and Tracey got a laugh out of that. I didn't have a problem with it, but I knew it was Lauren and Tracey who made it happen. Maybe it was for the best. I'd look for Dr. Matthews at my appointments hoping to get a good view of him down the halls, or around corners, but only saw glimpses of him at the clinic. Word was he was spending less and less time in the clinic and teaching abroad.

A year, two egg donors, and almost five very expensive cycles later, Maddie, Ben and I were not pregnant. I'd consumed a lot of medications and shots prior to each cycle to prepare my body and fluff up my uterus before pregnancy. I'd always become pregnant on the first cycle with surrogacy. It had always "taken" the very first time with first two-surrogacy journeys, which meant the transferred embryo would take to my uterus and implant on the first cycle.

I was exhausted. Adding to the exhaustion, I also became allergic to the progesterone shots, injected with a four-inch needle, which I used for twelve weeks for every cycle. I was sticking myself for nothing. I was so frustrated. It seemed the progesterone mixed with peanut oil was getting to me.

One day I was at Target with the boys and I was itching all over and didn't know why. I called the clinic as the red welts got bigger and covered more of my body. The doctor on call instructed me to purchase Benadryl and stop the shots. It immediately helped.

I had been okay with the meds because all of them were bioidentical except for the Lupron, which suppressed my own ovulation and I only took that sporadically.

At my next visit I asked Dr. Wrangler why the allergy happened because I'd never been and am still not allergic to peanuts. "Sometimes allergies to peanut oil just happen, and you never know why," he said.

"Maybe I just had too much progesterone in my system," I said thinking about all the damn shots I put into my body. I thought about Maddie and all she'd gone through, too, with her numerous failed cycles, and we both still did it all with no pregnancy, no baby to show for it. I really felt some of her pain, some of how it might have felt as an infertile woman unable to conceive. It made me want to help her more but the tired part of me was resisting.

Dr. Wrangler was moving around the exam room quickly and looking as if he couldn't wait to get out the door. I'm not sure if it was because I was the surrogate, or he just didn't have time for me that day. His schedule was intense, and the full waiting room confirmed my thoughts. I'm sure it was a little of both.

He changed my protocol to vaginal progesterone, handed me the new prescription, and said, "We'll move forward to the next transfer." I sighed a heavy sigh and he headed for the door. It was a signal to me our visit was done.

With his back to me I said, "Dr. Wrangler, I need to talk to you about this. My body is tired. Why isn't it working? Why are we not getting pregnant?"

I didn't usually talk to him much because he was always busy, but I was able to throw a few questions in now and then. I spoke up now because I thought it was important to figure this out. I almost felt ready to give up trying to get pregnant, and I didn't want to do that. I felt committed to Maddie, and Ben. I remembered their family photo albums at our first visit.

They were both devastated with the news of me not becoming pregnant and they didn't know what to do either. They were on their third egg donor! Something was wrong, and why was it always the egg. No one seemed interested in trying to figure it out. I wanted to somehow ask if anyone had done a checklist for them, and I was trying to figure out a way to ask Dr. Wrangler without showing any disrespect.

It was then he looked very seriously at me, with no expression whatsoever. "Have you ever thought it might be you?" Dr. Wrangler asked.

'Whoa, where'd that come from?' I thought.

"Well, no. No, I haven't. Could that be possible?" I said. "Would it be like some secondary, third, or fourth infertility? That doesn't seem likely."

"Well, it doesn't seem likely but I think it's possible," he said with a frown. "Maybe even lupus."

"Lupus!?" I said, surprised, and a little too loudly.

And then he turned and went out the door.

Lupus, with absolutely no symptoms? I thought about it while I was getting dressed to leave. Could it be true? Note to self: Google lupus. In his own way I could see he was reaching. But this time he was reaching too far trying to find blame in me.

I wanted to help my intended parents have a baby. Something was picking at my brain. "Why? Why?" I muttered under my breath on the way down to the lab to have my blood drawn, again. I felt like a pin-cushion.

I was always happy when I got the opportunity to talk to the embryologist, Dr. Doyle, when he drew my blood in the lab. He drew the blood when the lab techs were busy, and I learned a lot through him by asking lots of questions about embryology. He knew the subject fascinated me.

"Bummer, no pregnancy yet, Susan?" he said in his British accent. He looked British, and I adored his accent.

"No, but I guess we have to make it official with this lab test, right?"

"Yep, yes we do," he said as he made the poke into my arm. His unshaven face and uncombed graying hair gave him a gruff look, but he was too friendly to be that kind of guy. Even though his hair appeared messy, it looked like it should be that way, seemed natural. He started to draw the blood up into the tiny tube and I wondered how many blood draws I'd had as a surrogate mother.

Too many to count for sure.

"Dr. Doyle, I know it takes good genetics to make a baby. If the genes are bad and it's not the egg, but maybe something else, where does one go to find that out?"

"Karyotyping for sure, Susan. Sky karyotyping is a chromosomal color coordinator for DNA."

"Hmmm, interesting," I said. "Thank you."

When I got home I decided to Google it to death: Infertility. The whys and why not's. How does it happen? I Googled "genetics" along with "undiagnosed infertility" and "sky karyotyping," but as soon as I got into genetics it was way out of my league. I then hit the medical papers of genetics with karyotyping. As I learned, I wondered what specifically hadn't been done for Maddie and Ben. I didn't have their file so I could only make guesses.

I was at my computer for hours, days on end, searching and trying to find out what the issue was. Often I'd think to myself, 'Who was I to try and figure out why we couldn't get pregnant?' I was the surrogate, a womb for the baby, not a scientist. Yet, I kept on.

I emailed Maddie to see what type of testing had already been done and started a checklist. We used checklists often at work and I found them to be very helpful. Because we lived in different states, email and the phone were the best forms of communication.

Maddie replied back and gave me some information but finished her email with this: "Susan, don't take too much time on this. Let's leave it to the doctors." Then I read something in the email that struck me: "We've covered everything having to do with infertility."

I believed her but then I thought, 'what about genetics?' Did Ben and Maddie do any genetic testing in the past? In my next email to Maddie, I explained to her that during all four cycles of our failures, my pregnancy tests showed a faint positive on day 5 and 6, and negative on day 7 & 8.

"Something must be breaking down at that time. The pregnancy may want to hold, but it doesn't. Maybe something is chromosomally breaking down at that point and doesn't go on to make a baby," I wrote.

It was all starting to make sense to me, but I thought if I said anything that no one would believe me. You need good, healthy genetics to make a baby, or you won't have one. It was that simple. It didn't need to be complex. To me, it was crystal clear.

Maddie was the type to take in the information and thank me for it but she still seemed to have absolutely no hope. I could totally understand she was sick of it all, all this infertility shit. Maybe she was tired, too, like me?

Fuck.

Infertility sucks.

It seemed she couldn't put any hope in having a baby because no one was taking a personal interest in her case except her undereducated surrogate mother. I could tell she wouldn't believe a damn thing until her baby was in her arms. I could sense her arms were aching. I know it sounds crazy, but I could. What could she believe? She was so personally involved it was hard for her to see anything. She really stayed strong through this whole thing. I wished so hard I could be a sounding board for her, but I was sure Ben was there for her.

When I went for my blood testing before our next cycle, I asked to speak to Dr. Doyle again. I didn't have an appointment with him so I waited for close to an hour after the nurse drew my blood. Dr. Doyle was busy preparing embryos for another transfer.

I was happy to wait because it felt like we might be getting somewhere. When he came in to the lab, he sat down at the desk with me. There were partitions dividing the space for patient privacy. When he sat down he folded his hands together.

"Hi, Dr. Doyle, thanks for seeing me. I won't take up too much of your time. May I ask what genetic test would be the best to run if there are genetic chromosomal problems with infertility? Would it be like a specific karyotyping test, or…?" I asked.

He looked at me funny, wrinkling his forehead up like he was wondering why I would be asking such a complex question.

"Hypothetically speaking, yes. You can run a karyotyping blood test. But you can't do it here. You have to see a geneticist recommended by a doctor here for a complete blood work up. Believe it or not, it's typically covered by insurance. The results take fourteen days to come back," he said.

"I wonder if Dr. Wrangler would order it for Ben and Maddie if I asked," I said.

"Well, it's not something that is done very often, Susan. You have to schedule time with a geneticist to read the results to you, or whomever is tested. And because of the high possibility of things coming back unhealthy, or if there is a real genetic problem, it is usually irreversible and needs to be revealed by a trained psychologist to give that information to the patient tested," he said.

I nodded, knowing that there was a problem to be revealed. There just had to be. I didn't know enough to what it was. I'd read many medical papers about what might be wrong, things from Fragile X Syndrome to many other genetic issues.

"Thank you so much, Dr. Doyle, and especially, thank you for your time. I know you're a busy man. I guess we'll see how this plays out," I said. "See you soon." He got up after me, and I waved to him as I made my way to the lobby to go upstairs to the clinic for my appointment with Dr. Wrangler.

I went down the corner of the clinic to see Dr. Wrangler to get my uterus lining measured before the next frozen embryo transfer. I had one question, one particular thing to ask for, okay, beg him, to do: I wanted him to run tests for Maddie and Ben. It was the one thing that hadn't been done yet. The nurse brought me into the exam room while I waited for him. He walked in, said, "Hello," and sat down on the stool.

"Okay, let's get going." He proceeded to measure the lining of my uterus and said everything was ready to go. I summed up the courage to just ask.

"Dr. Wrangler, would it be possible to run genetic karyotyping for Maddie and Ben before this transfer?"

He looked at me like I'd lost my surrogate mind.

"Oh, come on, Susan," he said. He stood and put his hands on his hips. "You need to stop playing doctor and put your head into surrogacy."

Another zinger. Screw that. I decided to keep pushing to see if I could get what I wanted for Maddie and Ben.

"But, wouldn't it be worth a try?" I said confidently. "I doubt this transfer is going to work, Dr. Wrangler. The other four haven't. Can't we try something new, something that hasn't been done yet?"

He appeared to be a bit huffy again and stopped dead in his tracks and said, "Okay, Susan. I will do this test to humor you. I seriously doubt there are genetic problems, but I will have the genetic test run. Not right now, though. After this transfer," he said getting up from his chair.

He was angry and started to write in my medical file. It appeared he wanted to prove me wrong, and I was okay with that. I was happy. At least he agreed to it. I was pretty much done with it all anyway and would not have gone along with another transfer after this one. I had nothing to lose with making him angry.

"Okay, thank you. I don't know much, but I know this hasn't been done yet," I said to him as he left the exam room.

On our fifth attempt at a transfer, I again tested faintly positive on Day 6 after transfer, and negative on Day 7 and 8 with in home pregnancy tests. Five failed cycles with a surrogate mother!

I returned to the clinic after the blood test to confirm I wasn't pregnant.

A month or so later I returned for another appointment to talk with Dr. Wrangler about a new protocol for future transfers. I was sitting on the exam room table when Dr. Wrangler came in. His demeanor was totally different than all the other times before. He could not stop smiling. He had kept his word and did the genetic testing after the failed transfer. I wondered what was up and couldn't wait to find out what they found with the testing.

He smiled widely as he said, "There was indeed a genetic issue and it was a sperm issue, not an egg issue. We found the problem, Susan. This is huge for Maddie and Ben.

"Wow, that's amazing!" I smiled back at him, so relieved that they found the issue.

"I guess it humbled, not humored us all," he said, looking at me. He tipped his head down and looked up at me again. Now I couldn't stop smiling.

"I'm just happy we can move on with new information especially after what is it, a total of nineteen failed cycles for Maddie and Ben? It seems almost unbelievable they've gone through this much," I said and breathed in a new sigh of relief. It felt so good to know what the problem was.

I couldn't help but think that Dr. Wrangler had such a warm smile. When he smiled it complimented his whole face. His light blue eyes twinkled, and his bald head shined in the light. I started to see more of his character, of who he was as a doctor, and a man.

Dr. Wrangler let me know the genetic test showed the chromosomes would not work after a certain day of normal development, and testing on the embryo could not be done after a specific day. The cells would fizzle out when a fetus was trying to grow and develop.

"Mother Nature took care of it naturally by expelling and terminating the pregnancy," he said.

Ben could not father a child, and if he did by chance, it would create a baby with serious problems and/or developmental issues. The only way to fix the problem was to scientifically eliminate the fatal flaw out of the sperm. Dr. Wrangler explained that because all of the doctors had already tested the sperm, and it turned out healthy by other means and tests, they didn't think they needed a genetic test.

"Now we know," he said again.

"Yes, we do. It is really great news," I said. Both of us couldn't stop smiling.

"We'll get back to Maddie and Ben and see where they want to go with this new information."

"Okay," I said feeling relieved to not to go through another failed transfer.

I would come to learn over the years of working with the same clinic that they took credit for finding the issues with Maddie and Ben, which was fine with me. I found out the clinic would require future genetic testing on all new donors, and when they couldn't find a reason for unexplained infertility.

I didn't set out to make any big changes in the infertility world. I just wanted to help my intended parents become a family.

FIVE

JOURNEY #3 CONTINUED

Ben and Maddie took a few months off to figure out how, and if, they wanted to proceed with surrogacy. They were devastated by the news. First they said they did want to go ahead, but then they weren't sure. I told them I'd hang around to see what happened and stay with them for now. They were appreciative. I was faltering as well with my decision to proceed. I wasn't so sure I wanted to continue.

I was living in a new place with the boys after our landlord gave us notice he wanted to move back in to his home. We found a cute little beige house with an old bumpy asphalt driveway to rent on Second Street. It was an old home with character, and huge portrait windows in the back of the house that looked out onto the backyard. The floors were natural wood and higher than a normal floor. There were two bedrooms and one bath. Boomer had a big yard he could run in, and the school was nearby.

The owner, about my age, told me that the house was his "retirement dream." He would rent it out until he wanted to sell it, then retire. That gave me hope we wouldn't have to move out any time soon. Terrie and I parted ways as roommates because we couldn't find anything that worked for all of us, and she found a little apartment in the same city, not too far from us.

I continued to recover from all my body had been through with the hormones that prepared me for pregnancy. It was so nice not to have to remember medications every day, and not poke myself with that needle all the time.

Not only that, but I was dealing with a lot of my own personal hell as my mother had been diagnosed with throat cancer. She lived in northern California and needed someone to take care of her and drive her back and forth to the doctor for radiation and chemo. All of us siblings, my older brother and sister, and my younger brother lived far enough away from her that one of us would have to take her in to our home.

She came to me after she was diagnosed and asked if I could help. Since she came to me first, I invited her into our home until she got better. Mark my words, living with my aging mother as an adult and spoon-feeding her to keep her alive while helping her shower and go to the bathroom was one of the hardest things I've ever done. It was a living hell for her and me.

Kevin, my boss at work, was great when I told him I'd have to return to part time so I could take care of my mother. "No problem, Susan," he told me, "take care of your mother, and just get everything done for the manager workshops and report the hours that you work."

We were in the process of doing the workshops for hundreds of managers at the company, educating them about our new performance review software. I'd come in at night to set up the workshops for the next day and make sure all food and materials were ready to go. I'd be on call for anything Kevin needed in between. There was always something. I missed being at work full-time, and it was really hard taking care of my mom, being a mom and managing my job.

We put a twin bed for her out in the spacious living room near the huge windows. I'd ask her, "Mom are you okay?" She'd look at me with this unbelievably sick face that said, 'do I look okay?' As she was battling for her life, I doubted that I had any energy to continue with anything, including being pregnant, other than to take care of the boys, go to work, and care for my mother. It didn't seem I had any room left in my life for a surrogacy journey.

My mother quit smoking later in life after all of us left the house. She had been a smoker for decades, and a hard drinker of straight vodka for just as long.

I felt horribly guilty sometimes because as a teenager I used to tease my mother by saying, "Mom, for every cigarette you put into your mouth you lose a minute off your life." I was serious about it, though, and always hoped it would help her stop smoking. It didn't, and I'd always had an uneasy feeling that someday it was going to prove true, that cancer would find her. I truly hoped it wouldn't come true, but it did. I thought about my comment often because I had said it so many times to her.

As my mom's caretaker, I lost myself somewhere along the way. I'd see her as my mother, but because I was taking care of her 24/7, I felt like she had become my child. Our roles had switched, and I didn't want them to. I wanted my mother back. Sometimes I'd look at her face as she slept, and she looked like she was balancing precariously on the thin line between life and death.

I'd come to feel guilty and horrible about asking my mother to be with me during the selective reduction (abortion in utero) a few years ago with my second surrogacy journey when the triplets were reduced to twins. I know something died inside of her, too, that day, watching it happen. It still pulled at my soul, made me sad, and I felt incredibly guilty. I buried it deep inside, and I think she had, too.

My mom tried to follow everything I did with this surrogacy journey and kept a firm eye on me as best she could while she was ill. "Any babies yet?" she'd ask in a sweet, soft whisper as cancer was trying to take her. She was so good with babies and loved them like no other woman I'd ever known. She had a secret language with infants. I think it was the way she held them so close to her own body.

Fortunately, and gratefully, after nine months of treatment my mother survived throat cancer. While she was living with me,she had time to recuperate and came back to life. She became ready to move back to northern California to her own home. I know for sure it was incredibly hard on her being sick, and I also knew it was one of the hardest years of my life.

By the time my mother was getting better and was up and about at her own home, I received a notice from our land-lord that my rent was going up substantially. Rental prices were going up higher than they ever had been, and I would never be able to make the new rent. After a year at our new place, we would have to move. Again.

I found another home for rent in the same city. It was a three bedroom, two bath near the middle school, and there was a yard for Boomer! I was lucky this time because it was only about five blocks away so the boys could walk to and from school. It made my life a lot easier. I could go to work earlier as the boys didn't have to depend on a ride from me. Brian and Steven would have their own rooms for the first time. They were so excited. I hoped this would be perma-nent, but you never really knew for sure. I didn't want to be forced to move out of the beautiful beach city because the rents were unreachable. The school district was strict, and you had to live within the limits of the city to attend their public schools.

I found another new family online, a surrogate family. They were a large group of surrogate mothers who shared their experiences online. The group was formed under the name Surrogate Mother's Online, S.M.O,. It was a group full of thousands of surrogate mothers, some of whom had either gone through a journey experience or had multiple ones. Some women were there to learn more about being a surrogate. They were from all over the United States and a few abroad. It was a place to openly share information, and educate new surrogates on what others had experienced and what to look for in a journey.

When I shared my experience with the group, many knew who I was because of the Oprah article. Some felt sorry for me regarding that, and some did not like that I shared my story with the media because it shed a "bad light" on surrogacy. It's always like that — you're either for it or against it. Most surrogates had bad experiences when they shared a story with the media because the media was known to twist the story for the best drama they could get. I just happened to believe Oprah would be different, but she wasn't.

Overall, S.M.O. was a very good experience for close to five years, and I learned a lot. I shared frequently with a woman named Samantha who had been a surrogate mother twice. She lived in Kentucky and was married with three boys of her own. Her first journey was what is called a traditional surrogacy, which means the surrogate uses her own eggs and the intended father's sperm. Gestational surrogacy was what I did, which meant the surrogate does not provide her eggs, the eggs would be from the intended mother or donated to the parents.

Samantha always amazed me because in her second journey, she had given birth to two girls via traditional surrogacy using her eggs for the same family. They all remained close friends as the girls grew older. It was fascinating to me. I thought it was the ultimate form of giving.

I wasn't that giving. I knew that I could not use my own eggs and be a surrogate mother. There was just something inside of me that could not give away my own biological child. I marveled at the way she could do this and told her that many times.

"It's no different than gestational to me. Surrogacy is surrogacy," she often said when we talked about it.

Thankfully, I was too old anyway with my dinosaur eggs.

Samantha and I talked on the phone often and she provided wonderful support when I was trying to figure out if I wanted to continue being a surrogate.

"Why should anyone else decide for you whether or not you want move ahead?" she said. "It's your choice, Susan, don't let anyone make that choice for you."

I'm not sure why I needed that to be repeated back to me several times before I gathered the courage to proceed, but I was at my lowest low and my courage was zero. Samantha helped me pick myself back up and supported me through this down time. She had my friendship and my respect.

Right after we moved, Maddie called me and said she and Ben were ready to go for another transfer one more time. Some time had passed and they had decided how to build their family. At that point, I was ready and on board, and things in my life had settled down. I wanted to help them, and, hopefully, make their dreams come true.

I did my regular visit to the clinic and returned to full-time at work. I got the protocol for the transfer and took the medications like I'd done all the other times before. A few weeks later, it was the day before the transfer.

As I was putting away some of the last of the boxes after the move, Maddie called the night before the transfer.

"Please Susan, don't tell me if you do a pregnancy test, okay? I just don't want to know until we do the final blood pregnancy test at the doctor's office when you go in," she said.

My heart dropped a little, but I understood. She'd been through enough and didn't want to be on edge the whole time waiting wondering if it was positive. I wouldn't be able to share the good news with her early, but I got it. She knew me well enough to know I'd test no matter what. The home pregnancy tests could confirm the pregnancy way before the Day 14 blood test at the clinic. It usually took three to four days to get a positive test after a transfer depending on what day the embryos were transferred, and sooner with twins. The waiting time was crazy.

"Hurry up and wait some more" was a saying known in the surrogacy world.

I knew it was going to work this time, and we were going to be pregnant with twins, but I could keep a secret. I also knew once we were pregnant that she'd hold her breath for the whole pregnancy until her babies were in her arms. It was almost as if I had a movie camera in my head and it all played out well before the transfer. I visualized two babies, the ones they'd waited for so long. It was going to work.

Dr. Wrangler transferred two healthy embryos and he let me see them in the microscope before they were transferred. We'd come a long way with our doctor-patient relationship. This was my new favorite part of transfers. Ben and Maddie could not be at the transfer, but they sent a car for me to be picked up and brought back home after the transfer where I would do a two-day bed rest. It was Dr. Wrangler's typical protocol.

To my surprise they were present via telecom. It was so sweet to have them 'there' with me if just on a speaker.

"We'll both be at the first ultrasound, if there is one," Maddie said.

Now it was another two-week wait for them.

It was a five-day wait for me.

Pregnancy testing was a weird addiction with surrogates. No surrogate I ever knew waited for the blood test results at 14 days. We all tested because the home pregnancy tests were extremely accurate. We even had it down to a brand that would show an earlier result.

I home tested on Day 4, and got a very slight positive, but it wasn't good enough. I didn't trust it yet because it was so light that I could barely see it with a flashlight. I woke up early the next morning, about 4:00, to get up to pee, and tested again. The line was slightly darker, and I could see it without the flashlight.

Then I got the first real positive line on Day 5. Then again on Day 6, 7, and 8 + POSITIVE and it kept getting darker every day.

I had to wait another week before I could tell Maddie and Ben we were pregnant!! I didn't call her because I knew she would read the excitement in my voice. I didn't want to let on in any way that we were pregnant. It was the longest two weeks of my life, and I'm sure it was for them, too.

Our first ultrasound was one of the most joyful of my surrogate days. Their faces were so happy, so relieved and grateful they couldn't stop saying, "Thank you, thank you so much." It was the kind of happy I was at each of my first ultrasounds with my sons. Bewildered, blessed, and oh-so-excited.

It was the official start of our journey. Maddie had that look of concern when she thought no one was looking. Unsteady, worried in a motherly way thinking nine months was such a long way away. I'd find it was on all the faces of my intended mothers going forward. Because they weren't pregnant with their own babies, they felt out of control with what was happening. They didn't know what to expect with another woman carrying their baby.

It was a joyful look into my uterus with the vaginal ultrasound on our first visit.

"There is A and close by is B, both growing on time and healthy," Dr. Wrangler said, looking at Maddie and Ben with that same warm smile I'd come to know. Maddie started to cry. Ben hugged her, then out of nowhere Ben handed me a beautiful bouquet of flowers.

After my exam was done there was still so much joy in the room. It was time to leave and make a new appointment for the next visit.

"You are the proud parents of two healthy fetuses," Dr. Wrangler said proudly as he made his way down the hall to another patient. It was such a wonderful moment, one we had waited on for so long.

We made our way to the clinic lobby. They were so happy. I put my arm around Maddie and whispered to her, "Don't worry, I'll treat your twins just like they were my own, until they are in your arms." She hugged me and wouldn't let me go.

The whole pregnancy was uneventful and went along just fine except when it came to choosing an OB/GYN practice. I didn't feel fully comfortable going back to Dr. Kazman. Maddie and Ben were okay with that decision so they interviewed OB/GYNs for the twins. We stayed with Dr. Wrangler for the first twelve weeks and then moved over to our new doctor.

We found one we were happy with, and their office was also in Los Angeles. My biggest concern with the OB/GYN was that I wanted as natural a birth as possible with the twins without the possibility of C-section, unless it was an emergency. He agreed and said he'd delivered twins vaginally before.

Maddie and Ben made a few visits to Los Angeles during the pregnancy. Then they came for the next ultrasound when they started making plans for the nursery. When they arrived in L.A., they took time to visit with each of the boys, and with Terrie. We walked along the beach and shared meals together. We talked about almost everything. It was a real extended family kind of feeling with them.

On one visit while the boys and Ben were throwing the football around on the beach, Ben asked the boys, "So guys, what are your plans when you graduate high school?" Maddie and Ben were always interested in what the boys were doing, and how they were.

"Mom says we're going to college first," Steven said. "I want to go to college." Brian chimed in.

"I'd love to meet your mother, Susan. How is she, do you think she could make it to the twins' birth?" Maddie asked.

"Yes, she's doing very well, thank you. She'd love to come visit I'm sure. Thank you for the invitation. I'll make sure she gets it." I knew my mom, and that she'd love to be here for the twins' birth.

Visiting with them was always an adventure. Ben knew the boys loved sports so he'd take them out to throw around the baseball or football while Maddie, Terrie, and I would talk endlessly.

I was growing huge and the twins were healthy at every visit.

I had been employed at my job for about two and a half years, and I was about three months along with this third surrogacy journey. I'd proved myself during my temporary full-time employment, and my boss, Kevin, finally moved me to permanent status, full-time with better benefits. I was learning a lot, and it was amazing to me: this was the first job I'd really ever loved going to. I think it was because the opportunities for learning so many new things were endless.

Everyone that worked closely with me in HR knew about my story, but they didn't know that I was planning on doing surrogacy again. My belly was growing by the day with this twin pregnancy. I was eating out of control. I wasn't sure how to open up about telling people I was pregnant because it was so personal. I wished I didn't have to tell anyone. I hadn't been pregnant since I joined the company.

I kept it to myself as long as I could because I didn't want to have to explain everything to everyone, especially Kevin. He was happily married to a woman he met in college. I'd met her at a Christmas party, and they seemed to have a wonderful marriage of more than fifteen years, though they had no children. Kevin eventually shared they had fertility struggles with getting pregnant, and they opted to not have any kids unless they came in a natural way without fertility treatments. He also shared that his wife had two miscarriages during their marriage, and that was a hard time for them. Sharing these things with my male boss was pretty cool.

I told Kevin I was pregnant with twins. Even though I knew it was hard for him to understand being pregnant, he'd see me each and every day while I continued to get bigger, so I had to share, and I wanted him to be the first one to know. He was always very understanding of everything I needed to take care of regarding the pregnancy, as long as I did the job I was hired for.

Soon others at work started asking about my growing belly. "Are you pregnant again?" they'd ask. "How many is this now?" others would say. "Is this your first?" People who didn't know me would ask me around campus when they saw me. Sometimes they'd kindly stop me to make conversation as I was walking in another direction or at the elevator. People seemed to stop and talk to me more when I was pregnant than not pregnant. It was a funny thing, kind of an easy ice-breaker.

It was really hard to go into the long story with everyone, so I learned to cut it short, and just nod and say thank you a lot. When some people heard about "the surrogate" at work, I'd get random phone calls asking where they could go to find a surrogate. I referred quite a few people to different agencies in areas where they lived, and I'd hear back once in a while that it worked for them to create a family.

There was a well-meaning, very sweet older lady at work, named Edith. Her loving husband, already retired, packed her lunch every day, which always included a juicy orange. She was a year from retiring. She'd sit outside our office every day with her orange waiting for a report on how I was doing. Sometimes we would sit right there and other times we'd go to the company cafeteria for lunch. She'd pat my huge, growing twin tummy every chance she got, and she'd share her orange with me. I usually brought an extra one or two for me because they were something I craved during the pregnancy.

I craved orange anything, orange juice, orange cake, orange 50/50 bars, anything with orange. Edith desperately wanted to give me a baby shower, bless her heart. I told her why it really wouldn't be appropriate because I wasn't really expecting, my intended parents were — but she was hell-bent on giving me a baby shower because I was pregnant. I put the idea off continually when she tried to get me to pick some dates for the shower that were good for me.

"No, thank you Edith," I'd tell her in the sweetest way possible.

She finally gave up saying, "Okay, but I still think you should have one." She waved her arm in the air, not wanting to give in.

Along the way of sitting with her every day, we shared a lot of our own stories and got to know one another. It turned out Edith and her husband had their own story about infertility. For years they struggled to have a family and ended up adopting early on in their marriage. She adored her only son and talked about him all the time.

"I would have loved the chance to have my own biological child and do this surrogate thing, or at least have a choice in the matter," she said as she looked off into the lounge at the cafeteria where we sat. In reflection now, though, I probably wouldn't have changed a thing," Edith said.

I knew exactly what she meant.

SIX

JOURNEY #3 BIRTH

Maddie and Ben left the choice of which doctor to go to up to me after they interviewed other OBGYNs in the Los Angeles area. At that point, I didn't want to go back to my former OBGYN, Dr. Kazman, this time around because I felt bad that I didn't pick his friends to adopt the twins from my second journey. I didn't leave my last visit with him on a great note due to my decision for the adoption of the twins. I had told him it just didn't feel right with his friends. I didn't ever think that it would hinder another future pregnancy of mine.

And, now, I regretted my decision: The choice I made not to go to Dr. Kazman would cost me a C-section. I lost the possibility of a natural birth.

I had intended to have a natural delivery like I had with Dr. Kazman who delivered my first set of surrogate twins. It was the easiest birth I'd ever had at 45 minutes long. I thought it would be easy to find another doctor comfortable with delivering twins vaginally. I was wrong. In my opinion, some doctors, like the one we ended up choosing, cared more about liability than allowing a woman to have a vaginal birth.

Everything with the pregnancy was normal until I was 33 weeks pregnant. Our new OBGYN, Dr. Feinstein, told me after a regular pregnancy check-up that the ultrasound showed that the twins were developing differently. He said the condition is called "discordance." It means one twin takes nutrients from the other and becomes bigger while the other gets smaller.

"I can't completely tell you this is the case because with twins there are always some differences, and the ultrasound is never spot on with weights of the babies, but that is my diagnosis nonetheless," Dr. Feinstein said as he prepared an order for weekly progesterone shots to keep the babies intact.

I would have to go into the office every week to get the shots.

Of course, this worried Ben and Maddie. I could feel it in their voices on the phone and I would see it in their faces at every doctor visit we had in the following weeks. It brought discontentment and worry into our pregnancy experience. I'd never heard of discordance and it took me by surprise.

I felt at that point that Dr. Feinstein had already made up his mind to have a C-section instead of a natural birth.

"It might be time to deliver soon," he said a few weeks later. "I'd like to monitor you for a few more weeks but I do want you to have your intended parents come in with you as soon as possible so we can check the ultrasounds again."

Maddie and Ben had just arrived in Los Angeles and were staying at a friend's condo in Santa Monica they let them use for a few months. They were preparing for the babies' birth and getting things in order. They planned to keep them in Los Angeles for a few months until they were ready to go home and were unpacking when they got the call from Dr. Feinstein to come in for an appointment with me the next day to check the babies.

At the ultrasound the following day, we all were all surprised.

"How could this happen now?" Ben asked.

"It happens. There are always a few more complications with twins than a singleton," Dr. Feinstein said as he moved around my belly to measure the babies. He pulled the wand back and forth over my large belly stopping to measure everything as best he could.

"I think we should prepare for a C-section and deliver the twins within the next few weeks. There is an approximately 2.7 pound difference between the two, and the longer we wait, the bigger one will continue to take from the smaller one, and the smaller one will become too small and it will create problems," Dr. Feinstein said.

"Which one is the bigger one?" Maddie asked. She pulled one arm over the other with one hand over her mouth.

"The one on the bottom, the little girl." Dr. Feinstein said. She nodded.

"Well, to keep them both safe, we've got to do what we've got to do. But they are both okay right?" Maddie said. She looked over at Ben with concern.

Dr. Feinstein put his hand on my shoulder and looked over at Maddie. "Yes, yes, of course they are. We'll manage the situation on a daily basis." He said.

Ben and Maddie left the room so I could get dressed and Dr. Feinstein could finish up with me.

"Dr. Feinstein, about the C-section. I don't want one. I explained to you that I didn't want one early on. Is there any way to avoid this? I would much rather be induced and give birth vaginally if they need to come early," I said.

"C-sections are perfectly normal, Susan. I told you that. I just gave Britney Spears one. They are the in thing to do these days and it makes your schedule much easier because you can plan it," he said as he brought the stethoscope around to check my heart.

"I still don't want one. Is it possible?"

"We'll monitor it daily and see what happens," he said.

I was angry and felt betrayed. The fact that he gave one to a celebrity had no bearing on me. I didn't care about that. I didn't want a C-section, unless it was an emergency. It wasn't indicated and I didn't feel like it was medically necessary. It seemed to me the doctor was making a case for it simply because he wanted to do a C-section. I couldn't be sure because I wasn't a doctor, but it didn't feel right.

For a fleeting moment I thought about switching doctors and felt like running back to Dr. Kazman, but I knew I couldn't do that. Shit.

Dr. Feinstein gave Maddie and Ben a few dates within the next two weeks to choose from. Dr. Feinstein, Maddie and Ben looked at me as I lay on the hospital bed after all the testing at the hospital, as if to say, Please, let's just do this C-section. I wasn't sure who wanted it more, the doctor, or the intended parents.

I knew I had to have the C-Section. I mean, 'what happens if...' weighed heavily in my mind. What if something happened and I didn't agree to the C-section? There were too many what ifs to count. I was probably pretty whiny about it, but I hated the idea of being cut nine layers deep.

I ultimately agreed to the C-section because the what ifs were too risky. I immediately regretted picking an OBGYN I didn't know, even if he delivered for celebrities for status reasons. Looking back, I remembered an early conversation with Dr. Feinstein when he said, "Surrogacy always involves another party, and includes a lot of third-party liability. It's a slippery slope to manage," he said.

Oh well, lesson learned too late. I was too proud to admit I made a huge mistake. Little did I know then that this decision would affect all future pregnancies and put me in a high-risk category and that a C-section would be necessary for every future birth I'd have. Any future doctor I'd have wouldn't be able to consider a VBAC (Vaginal Birth After Cesaran) because of the multiple births I've had.

When it came time, Maddie and Ben picked a date from the options for twins' birthday. Maddie held my hand tight, and stroked my head during the whole frightful surgery, my first C-section. The moment the incision was made, I didn't feel it but I felt different. I knew I'd never be the same and tears came falling down my cheeks.

Maddie knew I didn't want the C-section and wiped away my tears with sympathy and reassured me that everything was going to be okay. It was a warm and touching gesture. She continued to hold my hand all the way up until her sweet twins were born.

Maddie couldn't see everything on the other side of the blue surgical curtain but she wanted to see her first baby being lifted from my womb. She got up on her tippy-toes to watch and see or hear that first cry. As she looked over the curtain, then at me, we both heard a faint cry that sounded like beautiful life music. The cry turned strong as the seconds went by.

"Go, go meet your beautiful babies. The nurses will take care of me." My teeth chattered together and I started to cry happy tears just like I did with all the babies I've given birth to.

She smiled and kissed the top of my head, and said, "Thank you, oh my God, thank you." She stood to the side and watched closely as Dr. Feinstein maneuvered their baby out of my body. She followed the nurse and couldn't wait to hold her baby.

Baby girl was born first. She weighed 7lbs 3ozs. Then a few minutes later her little brother, a little shy of 6 lbs, was born. It took him a little longer to cry but before long, he was just as loud as his sister. It wasn't bad for an early twin delivery, I thought. Baby boy was visually a little bit smaller. I was happy it was over and I didn't have to worry about the surgery any more. The babies and I were healthy.

I looked over to see Maddie and Ben wipe happy tears from their faces as they held their babies, and the looks on their faces were full of pure joy. The surprised, happy, new and amazing parents handed their babies over to the nurses so they could finish with them, and followed the nurses around while their babies cried. I often saw them glance at each other with looks like, Isn't this amazing? OMG!

Maddie was home. She had lost all of worry from her face. Her babies were with her at last after seventeen years of waiting. Ben was a new daddy and looked so proud. In my mind, this very moment made everything worthwhile.

I received a call from Maddie's mother while I was in the hospital a few hours after I delivered the twins. I'll never forget for the rest of my life the words she said to me, and how it made me feel. I was so proud.

She said, "Thank you, Susan. Thank you for making my daughter the happiest woman in the world. You gave her something no one else could. From one loving mother to another, thank you. You will always be part of our family."

I never expected a call like that from her mother. I cried happy momma tears.

Maddie had asked me a few months earlier to pump for the twins. I told her I'd be honored but I added a caveat that I wasn't a real good producer of milk. I barely had enough for my own kids and supplemented with formula. I told them I'd do what I could and as it turned out, I did pretty good.

It was hard work getting up twice a night to pump in addition to the daytime pumping. After a few weeks I was over it and felt done with pumping. But I made a promise of six to eight weeks. I was lucky to get eight ounces by the time Maddie or Ben came to my house to pick it up every day. Sometimes I'd have a little bit more. I'd get to sixteen ounces. I tried all the tricks, oatmeal and fennel, but nothing helped me except drinking tons of water.

Maddie and Ben called it "Susan's Champagne" because there was so little milk I produced at a time. They were grateful I took the time to do it. I was jealous of women who didn't even try to pump, who were overflowing with an abundance of milk and were able to stuff it in their freezers. I pumped for almost two months but it felt like a lifetime.

My recovery from the C-section went fairly well. It was a totally different kind of recovery than a vaginal birth, and much harder. I really hated it and ended up at the emergency department one night because the staples covering my incision came out when I reached for a dish in the kitchen. It was awful and there was a big puff of tissue above the incision that would not go down. I was frustrated with the staples because they didn't stay in place.

Dr. Feinstein said at my last postpartum visit, "It's all a part of the section recovery. Be easy on yourself."

I'd never see him again, that's for sure. I thought.

Before Maddie and Ben left for their home in Indiana they had all of us over for a few visits together. It was so wonderful to watch the twins grow those short weeks, to get updates on their eating habits, how they slept, and everything else about their babyhood. They were great hands-on parents. It was always a joy to see them.

It was a long journey, and I learned a lot. The journey was fantastic because we grew as friends but, the journey was over and it was time for them to move on. My job was done. The new family left a few weeks later for home and I couldn't help but think I'd probably not find intended parents like them again.

Those thoughts took me by surprise. 'Why would you be looking?' I questioned myself. I didn't have an answer for myself right then, and knew I had a lot of healing to do before I could even consider another journey. I wasn't looking per say but the idea of another surrogacy in the future might be something I wanted to do.

Over the next few months I'd receive updates that the twins were doing great, and it wasn't before too long that baby boy caught up in weight with his sister. I got many updates via email from Maddie and Ben. They'd send me notes of how the twins were growing and how their personalities differed. They traveled quite often, and they would put the twins on the phone and I'd hear babbling and coos up until they could talk a few years later, and then they'd say in the cutest little toddler voices, "Thank you for my birthday, Susan." It made my day and I always felt so proud.

We still keep in touch to this day, but less and less as the kids grow up. I know it's hard to keep in touch especially being a great distance from each other, but that's what happens as families grow and change. I know because my own family has changed so much over the years.

SEVEN

REFLECTION

The few months after the twins' birth was the hardest hormonal crash I'd ever had in my life. It was like a long, slow fall into oblivion. I was feeling signs of sadness that felt like depression, and I knew it was the hormones. I had no sexual drive what so ever, with a really dry vagina, but that didn't matter because my sex life was non-existent anyway. My energy was zero, and I wanted it back. Something. Anything. I called Dr. Feinstein's office and begged for some bioidentical hormones to help me through this time until my body started to get back to normal. He said exactly what every other doctor I'd had said after birth, "Give it time, Susan, give it time."

Since I had a little bit of experience with hormones with my surrogacy experiences, I mentioned to the OBGYNs after my last postpartum visit that hormones might help adjust me back. It made perfect sense to me because they give you hormones for many weeks before IVF when you prepare your body for the baby. Logically, why wouldn't they help the birth mother afterwards? It made perfect, logical sense to me. If I found a doctor that didn't care enough even to try new things, I wouldn't see them again.

No doctor would listen. I needed a doctor who would listen and be by my side.

Years later, and many doctors later, I found an internist who was well known in the Los Angeles area and had his own practice for thirty years. He specializes in bioidentical hormones and helps both men and women. He takes them himself and knows how much they matter as we age and as our bodies go through changes with hormones.

We'd had many conversations about hormones, so I asked him, "Why, why don't OBGYNs help women postpartum with hormones?" He said, "They don't care because it's not their specialty." He stopped and took a moment to look directly at me when he said this as he finished up my exam.

"That is so wrong. It can help so much," I said as I turned myself around on the exam table. "It can. I know how much it helps me. Some doctors just don't know," he said.

"Can women be addicted to these hormones, Dr. Leman?"

"Absolutely. It's a feel-good hormone for some." He turned his stethoscope around to listen to my breathing through my back. I breathed in, then out. "Right?" I said, still thinking about all of it. It just seemed so simple.

"Not all women, though. Some absolutely hate being pregnant. But there are a few that love it. One woman in particular, a colleague of mine, loved her pregnancy. I mean loved every minute of it, like you do. Everyone is different."

Spring was finally here in April, 2005. One morning after a shower, I was reflecting back on the day the twins were born. I was rubbing my hand over my almost healed C-section scar. I hated it, it made me sick. It also made me mad.

The doctor said it would heal and go away, but it never did. No one told me that I'd end up with a little flab of tissue over the seam of the scar. I researched it as much as I could and found that it was pretty common for women to hate their scars and all women healed differently. Some women didn't mind their scars; they were thin and didn't have the puff of tissue at the top. Some even said their scars were barely noticeable. I wished mine was that way.

I thought about doing surrogacy again but really had no idea how to match because I knew I would not go back to Lauren and Tracey's agency. Nothing really happened to make us split up again, but I didn't feel comfortable going back to them. Our business relationship ended, and our friendship probably never started. I thought we were friends, though distant, but we really weren't.

I wanted to do a surrogacy without Lauren and Tracey. I could do all of the things required with the other professionals like the legal end and the medical appointments myself. I didn't need a third party. I started thinking about all the pros and cons for another surrogacy. At the top of my list was:

PRO –

#1: If I do another surrogacy, it's inevitable that I will have to have another C-section, so, in the second one it should fix the half an inch tissue at the top of the scar that puffs up. I was certain this wasn't the way the scar was supposed to heal.

CON –

#1: I would have to go through the postpartum process again.

#2: I would have to try to find a match myself.

I only got as far one item on pro, and two on con. I didn't know anyone personally looking for a surrogate, and trying to find intended parents via Surrogate Mothers Online (S.M.O.) was few and far between, but it could be done through their classified ads. Many surrogates found matches that way.

I thought about starting early so I could find intended parents that I could get to know better, and maybe intended parents like Ben and Maddie. I started drawing up what I wanted in intended parents, and what I wanted out of surrogacy in general, then I started working on a classified ad. It was the only way I'd find a match.

My ads always started out with "Experienced Surrogate Mother," and sounded like I was selling my services, offering up my womb — and I was. There was no way to get around it. That's exactly what I was doing.

I thought about the Oprah experience and how renting a womb was starting to apply. Even though I didn't care for the play on words, or the label, I saw how other people could see it that way. I never viewed it quite that way before.

I wasn't sure how to get around that type of ad. Various newspapers would not allow surrogacy to be advertised so there was no way of advertising for surrogacy services except through Surrogate Mothers Online.

I've always felt that receiving compensation for being a surrogate mother was well-founded and right. I haven't wavered from that point because it is, indeed, hard work to be pregnant for someone else and it involves a lot of time.

The times have changed for surrogacy these days. They are starting to work "pre-birth child support" into the contracts for compensation. It works a lot like pre-birth orders when parents get their names directly put onto birth certificates. Everything is planned ahead and well thought out.

Surrogate friends of mine and I were some of the first ones to use this terminology in our contracts. They used to list surrogacy compensation as "pain and suffering." There is a give and a take for it, too. Because it takes work, it also involves your family support and help. They also give up a lot when and if complications arise.

I got to the point where I just let surrogacy be. I would get all the way to where I would finish an ad, and I just couldn't list it. I wasn't fully ready to move forward, but I left the opportunity open. My life was full with the boys, work, and everything else.

I dated but nothing was fulfilling. I kept meeting married men, practically like a magnet, on Match.com. I started looking other places so that I would find people who were open to starting a relationship.

I signed up with a place called "It's Just Lunch." It was a dating service so I paid their fee to see where it might go. I figured it might weed out the married men and the men not looking for a real relationship. 'Actual single men might be on it' I thought.

As it turned out, they should have renamed it to "It's Just Women." Many men had told me during our dates, "I have three, even four dates a week if I want it. I'm always dating." I was lucky to get one date a month. Seriously. And that was only if I was lucky! I found out weeks later that the site was flooded with single women and very few men.

One guy asked me out twice. I said yes to the second date, and about fifteen minutes in he said to me, "So, are you into tantric sex?" I barely knew what it was, but it piqued my interest even though I hardly knew the guy. He actually had a little creepy side that I couldn't figure out. Whenever I felt that creepiness, I knew it wasn't right for me. Then he told me I looked like his ex-wife.

The date was over.

My dating life was so ridiculous and somewhat hilarious that it became a thing of interest at work. Two women who worked in another department, Janice and Emily, would always love to hear my dating stories. They'd grab their tea or coffee during a break or I'd I go into their offices after lunch where we would share and update each other about our lives.

"So, Susan, any new dates lately?" one would eventually ask, and they'd both lean in with their coffee cups to hear everything.

The last date I told them about was a guy through It's Just Lunch. "Okay, so this one guy was cute. It seemed he had everything going for him, right?" They nodded their heads. "And..." they'd say, egging me on.

I told them that after the basic introductions, we were getting to know about each other's family. I gave him a short run down of the boys and he started telling me about his kids, two boys who were now in their late teens to early twenties. Then, just five minutes into the date he said, "I have a ton of guns. I keep them all at my son's house. He's on house arrest so he looks after them for me. I have an arsenal fit for an army!" He was so excited, like it was the best thing in the world to have a lot of guns. He said this to me, someone who doesn't own a gun and doesn't really like guns at all.

We'd just ordered our food at lunch, but I immediately started getting a serious stomachache. I'm sure my face looked like a deer in the headlights of an oncoming car. I wanted to just slip away somehow and be gone from the date, and then realized I just ordered lunch and would have to wait for it, and eat it in his company. I wasn't sure he wasn't totally putting me on, but I didn't know. He seemed sincere.

As I explained all this, I felt so naïve. Janice and Emily died with laughter as I told the story. I told them the date was actually pretty scary because the guy just kept on talking about guns. I'm not sure they knew I was serious because they were still laughing.

I told my date that I had to leave because I wasn't feeling well, then I went up to the counter, told the waitress that I'd like my food to go, paid for it and left. The restaurant had large picture windows all the way around the building, so when I left I recalled hoping he didn't get a look at the license plate on my car from the window where we were sitting. It was creepy. It was crazy.

Janice and Emily tried not to laugh but said, "It's funny, Susan! We're sorry we are laughing, we know it's hard these days, but what an unbelievable story!" Janice said. I agreed, but, oh my God, I couldn't get a break with dating. I felt like me and my life was a laughing stock.

That evening, I was so close to emailing Adam. It'd been a little over two and a half years since I saw him. I was incredibly lonely but knew calling my married former lover would make me feel like shit in the long run. I'd come so far to forget him, but I was an expert at ignoring that it was wrong to contact him. I struggled to not contact him. I thought about it a lot and wondered if I still loved him or if he was just convenient for me. It wasn't love. Or maybe it was.

How could I be this screwed up? One thing I knew for sure was that he didn't love me the way I loved him. I mean, seriously, it was impossible because he was married. I forgot that, too, conveniently, but when I again reminded myself that he was married, I didn't call him, and I stayed strong. I started to hate that I loved him still. 'How could I get rid of that?' I thought.

I made an appointment for a massage instead of calling him because I didn't want to start all over again and keep making the same mistakes over and over.

The next morning, I was up getting dressed for a celebration of life for the father of the mother of my second couple, my second journey, and my first set of twins. This couple were the intended parents that adopted the twins and were named Kathy and Russell. Kathy's father had just passed away, and they were having a celebration of his life.

I didn't dress up very often; getting 'dressed up' meant I put a dress on. It was supposed to be a big celebration with hundreds of people invited. I'd get a chance to see my first set of twins who were just ending the toddler stage.

I went by myself to the celebration because the boys were either over at their dad's house that Saturday or maybe baseball practice. It was set for 1:00 p.m. and was meant to go well into the evening. It was so nice to get out again, even if it was by myself.

As I made my way through the crowds at the celebration I didn't know many people, only Kathy, Russell, and their immediate family, her mom, sister, and the kids.

Kathy came up to me with the twins right when I got there. "Susan! Hi!" The twins were all smiles, all dressed up, and running all over the place. I got hugs from everyone and noticed how fast the twins were growing.

Kathy was sad about her dad passing away, but happy that he lived such a good life. He wanted them to celebrate his life. There were many tears and a lot of friends. Kathy introduced me to many of her friends, and I mingled a bit here and there while I was playing with the twins. We were playing hide and seek around the dance floor.

About half way through the celebration, Kathy walked up to me holding hands with a petite blonde woman, and a tall man followed them. She walked up to me as I was playing with the twins.

"So here is our angel, Susan, who birthed our twins," Kathy said to the two people standing with her. "Susan, this is the couple, Dave and Bev, I told you about a few months back. Bev is in my infertility group. They've tried to have a baby quite a few times and have finally given up, and they might need a surrogate mother."

"Oh, I see." I remembered her telling me a few months back but wasn't sure anything would come of it at the time. People were dancing all around us as we moved to the side of the dance floor to continue talking. The twins were running up to me tugging on my dress wanting to play.

Dave was tall, with broad shoulders and light brown hair. He said, "We saw you playing with the twins, we know your whole story, and it's really sweet how much you love them." I smiled back at Dave and Bev. "Thank you," I said above the music.

Bev leaned in to say something, but I didn't quite hear her through the music. We eventually moved to the side to sit at one of the tables and talk. We talked most of the party. They told me all about their baby-making failures. They'd been married eight years, and said how very much they wanted a baby, even just one baby.

Dave was studying the bar to be an attorney, and Bev was the manager of a large medical group. Bev had a really elegant, vintage look about herself. It might have been her blonde hair parted on the side with curls close to the head, styled like a 1950s movie star. They were just like any other people you meet, and most people would never know they were struggling. I could see how hard it was for couples struggling to have a baby, though. Everyone had a story, and as a surrogate mother, I ended up hearing many, many different stories about infertility.

"It's so amazing that you have such a kind, giving heart," Bev said. I smiled and felt a little out of place. I felt I was just like anyone else. I just so happened to love being a surrogate mother.

I warmly smiled again. "Thank you. It gives me back so much more, Bev," I said as we continued our conversation over drinks. "Sometimes I truly can't find the words to express what it gives me in return." I meant it because sometimes literally there were no words for how I felt.

She smiled and said, "I'm sorry if Kathy was a little short about our introductions, but we were wondering if you might consider carrying again, for us, maybe? Are you thinking about doing surrogacy again by chance?" She asked with her eyebrows raised, waiting for an answer.

"Actually, I have been considering it. Thank you, I'm honored you asked," I said. Beneath my calm demeanor of being a confident surrogate mother was the self-doubt and oceans of fear. The "What Ifs" started to creep in.

What if I don't do as well as I did in the past? What if they aren't like my last intended parents? What if I don't get pregnant again? What if I have to have a C-section again?

Here they were offering me the position that I thought I wanted. Again, here it was, right in front of me. Then I thought about work. How would they take it? I sighed long and loud to myself.

"I'll definitely let you know after I figure a few things out, okay?" I said. They were perfectly fine with my answer. I could tell she really wanted an answer, but I really needed to think about it in depth before I made a commitment.

I thought about our potential match more on the drive home. The good thing about it would be that it is a friend of a friend, not a stranger. That made a difference for me. I liked the fact that I could help someone who knew someone that I knew.

A few days later on a Friday night, the boys weren't home, and I was sitting in front of the computer thinking about what diet I needed to go on to lose that last ten pounds after the pregnancy with the twins. I was back at work and there were a few pairs of pants that still didn't fit. I don't wear tight pants; it does not feel good when you sit at a desk all day.

I was always lucky to bounce back and get into most of my clothes for work, but for some reason this time it was tougher. I didn't have the extra money to go splurge on new clothes. Kevin, my boss, was happy I had returned, and I was getting back into the work groove. I was starting to feel a little better with the hormone fall off, too.

I opened up some chocolate-chocolate chip ice cream and grabbed a spoon. I had plans to eat the whole pint, which definitely wouldn't help with my weight loss. Then I started to Google my ex-boyfriends. (I've done this before, of course, who hasn't, right?) Into the second hour of searching, it felt like I had some reason to do this.

At first, I had just been randomly surfing. I thought of the boy who first kissed me when I was thirteen going on fourteen. It had taken me by such surprise, and I don't think anyone ever forgets their first French kiss. It was a mix of it seeming to be magical, then honestly, it was kind of gross. I loved the thought of being kissed, but my still young brain thought it was kind of yucky. Bobby Martinez was his name. Bobby was two years older than me and got his girlfriend at the time pregnant when we were in high school. Another one to stay away from, my intuition had said. I listened then, too, thank goodness.

Then I went up in age, back to the first guy I had sex with, Scott. I met him when I was a senior in high school. He would end up taking me to prom, which I barely remember even attending. We knew how to party like the best of them with alcohol and drugs. I was just about to turn eighteen. I'd like to say I made love to him, and probably at the time I wished it was love, but it wasn't. It was plain old boring sex. I remember thinking afterwards, "Is this it?" All my friends made sex out to be such a big thing, that moment you change from being a girl to being a woman. I guess I felt like a woman afterwards only because my friends said I was, but to me, it just wasn't that big of a deal.

Strangely enough, Scott contacted me years later when I was in my mid-thirties, right after my divorce. He wanted to see if we could give our relationship another try. Wait. What? We had 'a relationship'? That was news to me. He said he found me through my high school reunion information in Oceanside, California. (Facebook wasn't alive yet.) He got my email online and wrote to me. "Do you think we could get together again to see if 'we' might work?" he said in the email.

My first reaction got my ego started and it said, "Hey!! What do you know? He came back!" Then I got over myself and realized that this guy needed to stay in my past. He wasn't any good for me. But then my mind began spinning a bit. Maybe he'd changed. I'd always hold out hope for other people. I'm not sure why, but I'm sure it's something from long ago.

Scott was the ultimate surfer man/boy at twenty-two that was destined to never stop surfing, like ever. He had the erect stiff back you get from sitting on your surfboard too long, and shoulder length blonde bleached out hair from the ocean water. He was always surfing and everything that decorated his tiny apartment was surf related. Here is what I remembered as I walked down memory lane with Scott.

When I was eighteen, just after we'd slept together, I went over to his apartment to surprise him one night. I thought we were dating each other, and so that was the thing to do, spend time together. Terrie, my close friend, happened to be with me so we went to his place so I could introduce her to him. I knocked on the door.

Scott opened the door two inches and said, "Hey, hi, I can't see you tonight." And shut the door again. After about five minutes of me pounding on his door, he opened it again about two inches and said, "I have someone with me, a woman I met at the bar tonight. Sooo, can't see you. Bye." He slammed the door quickly in my face.

I was devastated and demanded that she leave. He wouldn't let me in. I again demanded she leave and kept pounding loudly on the door. I was going to make their night awful for them. Terrie moved away back by the top of the driveway from where I was.

"Susan, it's not going to work. Come on, let's go," she said.

Then Scott opened the door and said, "Move away from the door so she can leave." It was so embarrassing, and I was making a complete idiot of myself. I backed off and moved over by Terrie as the woman left his apartment.

After she left I broke up with Scott right on the spot right in front of Terrie. I then announced Terrie and I were going over to crash a party next door.

"I wouldn't go over there if I were you. It's a bachelor party," Scott said as I walked past his two surfboards and right on down his dirt-paved driveway two blocks from the beach in Carlsbad.

I didn't react very well to his comment. I was a broken-hearted barely eighteen-year-old just about to graduate high school.

"Don't tell me what to do. You lost that privilege. Fuck you!" I said when I hit the end of his driveway. They were the last words I said to him until he contacted me via email.

I was angry, and unbelievably hurt even though he was not my type. And he wouldn't be the last man I cried over. There was a reason we didn't work out and never had a real relationship.

Terrie and I went straight to that bachelor party — and left shortly thereafter. He had been right. The scene was true life bachelor party, with naked girls dancing on table tops, and many unruly, drunk men who mistook Terrie and me for dancers. We didn't feel safe and left immediately. It was clearly dangerous.

There were lots of tears that night. My muffled cries went into Terrie's kind shoulder. We were always there for each other and remain so to this day.

So, it truly was a surprise that Scott found and contacted me. He said, "I'd love to see you again. I have a successful construction company on the Big Island and you can come here to see me," he wrote in the email. He wanted me to meet up with him in Hawaii sometime, or at the Los Angeles Airport because he was flying there to make another connecting flight. It got my attention, but my intuition said, 'Run, run as fast as you can. He's not for you.' I thought of how our paths had already crossed and didn't sense there was any future together. I didn't want to meet up with him and told him we were a thing of the past.

Many people, mostly men, and some women, say women's intuition is a myth. I was learning that womanly intuition is not to be fucked with, and when you listen with close attention, She (intuition) is usually right on.

EIGHT

MOTHERLY LOVE

I was at my mom's two-bedroom apartment in northern California surrounded by tall trees on every side of the huge, multi-building apartment complex. The trees had to be two stories tall and were just beautiful. There were many birds and colorful flowers in the landscaping around the trees.

I had gone to visit my mother to see how she was doing after all the cancer treatments, and to help her with some computer issues. She was doing great and getting stronger, and it was so wonderful to see that she had beaten stage four throat cancer. The doctors said that if she hits the five-year mark cancer free, that it would be a good sign.

In her apartment, one bedroom was for sleeping (her room) and one was for sewing. My mom was very crafty, and she had material stacked on tables and crafts all over the place in that room. I'd always admired her skill and patience in sewing, crocheting, crafting. You name it, or show it to her, and she could make it. It was what she did so well. This ultimately led her to working at a store like JoAnn's Fabrics as a store clerk specialist. People would seek her out to help them with their projects, asking other employees, "Where is the tall lady with silver hair who knows how to do stuff?"

She could crochet a blanket overnight. Her sewing skills were amazing, too. For whatever reason, I did not inherit those skills. I had searched since I was a little girl to find something that I was good at. I loved to write but it never went anywhere. I thought I had found something I really loved doing: Growing babies was something I was really good at, but, I couldn't do that forever.

It was my last day visiting, and we decided to go to a nice meal before my flight that evening. My mom seemed particularly antsy, the way she was when she wanted to tell me something. I ignored it because I was starving, and a hungry me will always get particularly whiny whenever I need food. We decided on P.F. Chang's. One of my girl-friends and I would have a cosmo and talk girl-talk at the one close to my office after work now and then. Their food was always great, and this particular restaurant had dim lights and bright, deep red votive candles all around. It had a nice ambience.

After my cosmo arrived and the waitress walked away, my mother finally looked at me and asked, "Are you thinking of doing surrogacy again?"

"Yeah, I was thinking about it," I said to her as I picked up my drink. "I figured you had something to say to me,

Mom. You know you're my biggest advocate with surrogacy, and you can say anything to me," I said as I took a big gulp of cosmo. It was a perfect mix of chilled vodka and cranberry, and it tasted so good.

"I'm concerned you are doing this too much, that it might hurt your health in some way," she said, sipping her water. "You've already helped a few families, Susan." She put down her water and rested her hand on the table. I noticed my mother's hands had started to change. She had a few more white age spots on them. I looked back at her.

"Mom, I could find a hundred reasons why I should or shouldn't do it. But the fact that I can do it, and that it's something I do really well makes me want to do it again," I said looking at her.

Deep down I knew she was right, that it was probably time to stop, but I didn't want to. I was like an alcoholic who wants that next drink. No one can tell them that they can't have it. They just know they want it, and maybe they are even convinced they need it.

I couldn't believe I made that comparison and kept it to myself. I did want to do it again, and it definitely helped out financially. It was helping me put some funds away for college for the boys.

My mom was concerned about me being pregnant all of the time. Fair enough. She went on to tell me she didn't know of anyone else who had this problem, wanting to be pregnant all the time. She felt it was getting out of hand.

I started to laugh a little bit at the absurdity of it all. She added, "Susan, it's not funny. You could die." I stopped laughing and looked at her. "Mom, I am doing it again. I've already found a couple to work with. They're good friends with Kathy and Russell."

She still wasn't convinced it was a good idea and glared back at me knowing I was going to do what I wanted to do. I was sure she must have had a bad dream about it or had talked to other people who added their opinion about her surrogate daughter. She gave me her most disapproving motherly look. Man, I hated that look.

I could tell from her tone that she wasn't mad. She was just very concerned, which made me feel a little uneasy. My mother was the sort of person who would always tell her kids, my older brother, older sister, and younger half-brother, when she was concerned about something that involved our health.

"One more, Mom, I swear that's it. One more," I said, thinking about hearing her voice say the same thing in my mind as a little girl when she'd take a drink. She herself had had a tough life being a chronic alcoholic; she would drink vodka straight from bottles, not bothering with a glass.

She went to outpatient alcohol rehabilitation twice, thirty days each, before she could stay sober when we were little, leaving us with a predator stepfather. My mom drank for a million reasons throughout her life, and finally quit when I was thirteen. I'm sure if she had not quit then she wouldn't be alive today.

Mom had been pregnant with the four of us, had had four miscarriages, and had one daughter who lived for just ten hours before dying in her arms because she was born too early. I know my mom was worried about that possibility, and worried about me.

The risk as a surrogate mother was real. But I felt strong and knew myself well enough to know things would be fine. We'd been through so much already, and I know she didn't want me to be hurt. That's what good moms do: they try to get you not to do things that might hurt you.

Since that time, and all through the lifetime of hurt, hers and mine, we made amends and now had a better relationship than ever before in my life.

I wanted to tell her I was going to have a transfer of embryos in a month with Bev and Dave, but I couldn't. I just couldn't. And that Bev, Dave, and I had decided to go the "independent route" which meant we didn't have an agency to handle things. I was okay with that, and it saved Bev and Dave a huge agency fee.

I wanted to tell my mom that my doctor was kind of being sketchy about approving future pregnancies, that he seemed so one-sided. I knew he'd be professional about it if I asked, but his opinion was getting in the way. This time we didn't need doctor approval because we weren't using an agency.

I'm sure mom was more worried about my age than anything else. I wasn't. I felt strong and determined that I could carry another pregnancy without problems even with my age. I didn't take any medications and my health was excellent. Then it finally came, the comment that pissed me off.

"You are no spring chicken, Susan." Then she added, "You're almost fifty." I had just turned forty-five. I gulped down the rest of the cosmo and didn't say anything.

"Mom, seriously," I said stuffing food into my mouth. "I wouldn't do it if I couldn't. Age really has nothing to do with it. I'm healthy, and if age was a factor, I wouldn't be able to be a surrogate, they wouldn't approve me."

She knew me well enough to know I would go ahead with it anyway. There were no reasons why I shouldn't except for fear, and I wasn't signing up for that.

I looked down at my phone to see a missed call from Brian. It was probably to find out when to pick me up from the airport. I remembered that my landlord recently sent a letter to me and I hadn't answered him yet. "I forgot to tell you, Mom, I have to move again. Can you believe it?"

"What?" she replied.

I stopped eating so I could fill my mom in on the story. I was so fed up with all the moving I've done since I've lived in this city. I pulled my napkin from the table and put it over my mouth.

"Our landlord, this new one, is raising our rent. It's happened to us almost every year or two. And now, again. God! I can't get a break and will be moving once I find a place. I put in an application for a place last week. It's next to the city we live in now, and the rents are cheaper, so we'll just see what happens I guess."

I couldn't afford the raise in the rent. It wasn't just a little increase, it was an $800.00 a month increase. I hoped I could find a house close by, at least close enough for the boys to attend the same school. A simple, everyday home like the one we lived in was going for close to a million dollars. I wasn't anywhere in the running to purchase or rent a home in this beautiful beach town.

My mother and I usually lasted together two or three days max, then we'd get on each other's nerves, and so it was time for me to go home. I know she meant well, and she looked much more relieved after she told me what was on her mind. She was worried about me. I loved her so much.

There is a special place for mothers. It's like when you look at them and know that you are a part of them, and they are part of you, and no one can change it. It's a deep connection of knowing they will always be there for you in a human way no matter what happens. Later in my life, I'd make that same kind of connection to nature, the veins in a leaf on a tree were like pathways to the lungs in my body. The ocean water always renewed my sense of being, like a place from once I came. I could go on and on, it was all about connection.

After my mom dropped me off at the airport, I sat down and stared out the large windows, watching planes land and take off thinking and thinking about my life. One thing I knew for sure was how to be a mom. I also happened to know how to grow babies and give birth relatively well. I had a great job, and had a lot going for me. I wanted to share it with a special person. I thought about how Brian and Steven were older now and would be off to college in less than a few years. I thought about it often, and wanted to live in, relish every moment while I still could.

NINE

JOURNEY #4 START

We were ready to move forward on our journey and complete all the things we needed to do before transfer. Bev and Dave were excited to get things moving, and I was ready because we were doing all of this ourselves, without an agency. They knew some of the procedures, and what they didn't know I filled them in on. We did the legal paperwork and all the other things we'd need to move it forward.

It was so easy to work with both of them and we agreed easily on everything. We basically used a template from my last surrogate contract and had the same attorneys from the last journey put in the new information. Bev and Dave had frozen embryos so we wouldn't need to go through the egg retrieval process, which made it much easier to schedule a date for transfer.

We were a few days from signing contracts when Bev and Dave invited me to lunch. We met at a quaint little restaurant in Los Angeles that I'd never heard of. Bev went there often. It was painted yellow, full of lush plants and colorful pillows on the chairs. Our table was tucked away into a little corner. It looked inviting and I was excited to go and talk over the last few items with them.

"Susan, um… I have a concern," Bev said to me about fifteen minutes into our conversation. I was a little worried because it sounded like it might be a deal breaker of some kind.

"I think I told you about a psychic I use every now and then, right?" I nodded my head and remembered Bev talking about this person she saw in the past. I believed it was a personal preference to use someone like that to guide you in life. This was something of a life coach, but on a more spiritual plane of guiding one through times of trouble or to help you through a situation. She went on to explain to me that she's known this person for a very long time, and they had an established relationship.

"I'll just get right to it," Bev said. She had my full attention and it sounded really serious. I stopped eating and she looked hesitant like she didn't want to say what she was going to say.

"My psychic does not believe you are the right surrogate for us," she said. Her face was serious, her blue eyes intense. She brushed away wisps of blonde hair from her face.

I was shocked and I didn't know what to say. I put my fork down.

"She thinks, after I showed her your picture, that you are not to be trusted with our baby," Bev said flatly, waiting for me to respond. I said nothing, sitting with my hands in my lap. I was still chewing my salad very slowly wondering what picture she showed to her, thinking, 'do I look that bad? Like someone who isn't to be trusted? What picture was it?' Apparently, her psychic didn't get good vibes about me, whatever the photo.

I said, "Okay..." hesitatingly nodding my head. A lot of things were swimming around in my mind, but hurt feelings came to the surface first. This was not the way to start a journey, but this was someone she respected and always gave her fair and honest advice about what she asked.

"Um, we don't have to proceed if you aren't comfortable," I said. "We don't have anything officially started in this journey yet, and haven't signed contracts, so we can just walk away at this point if that's what you guys want." They looked at each other.

"Well, it's not that we don't trust you," Dave said. "It's someone Bev trusts and admires and has helped her a lot throughout her life." Dave moved around in his seat uncomfortably. I moved uncomfortably as well because I didn't know what to say.

"You can choose someone else to carry for you, someone your psychic approves of," I said. I thought our match was done and I didn't know where they were going with this information. It sounded like there was a lot more to the conversation than I was privy to.

I wondered what this psychic said to Bev. Whoa, did I wonder. I can't remember exactly what Bev said after that, but it was along the lines of not being trusted. I thought, 'Jeez, if I haven't proved that I can be trusted through all I've done to get us to this point already, as well as my successful journeys, then maybe we really shouldn't proceed.'

I was glad that Bev came forth with it because earlier I could tell something was bothering her. I'm sure it took a lot for her to tell me. She respected this woman. I didn't know what she wanted me to say to her, and yet I couldn't help feeling offended. I tried to keep an open mind, and I knew for sure I did not want to proceed unless they - and I - were perfectly comfortable.

Bev reassured me that maybe she heard the psychic wrong, but the damage had been done. It wasn't clear why Bev told me. Did she want a particular reaction from me? Maybe she was questioning herself about going forward, and she did what she thought was right.

It was true I didn't know them very well, but I didn't really have to know them well for a surrogacy journey. I did know that we absolutely needed to agree on things before we started.

Then I remembered how I thought I knew my first husband after I'd been married to him for ten years and after dating him for five before that. By the way he acted after our divorce, I clearly never knew him at all. I thought I did. You can know someone for years, and never really *know* them.

Bev, Dave, and I had a few months of serious talking. I don't remember all of the specifics, but I was not going to start something I wasn't comfortable with. Some of the closeness and emotional connection I felt with them was gone. It felt a little more like a business transaction, working toward the same goal. It could have been because we took care of the financials of the journey, too, which made it feel more business-like as well. We finally all agreed on what our journey entailed, signed contracts, and started to plan for the transfer just after the new year in 2006.

The last thing I remember telling Bev was, "I'll carry your baby just like I would my own." And that was the truth.

Maybe she just needed that reassurance? I'm not sure if she decided to proceed just because we'd already put so much into it, or that maybe she talked to her psychic again. I'm not sure because it never came up again. They weren't my past-intended parents. They were my current intended parents, and I was finding that every single journey I went on was different from the previous ones. Just like friends, the connections were all different.

After the embryo transfer, I stood over the toilet waiting for the pregnancy test to turn positive. I could feel the hormones swirling around my body. At that particular moment I doubted my pregnancy because I felt the hormones were messing with me. It'd happened before with Ben and Maddie. First I thought I was pregnant, and then I wasn't. It was so weird how the hormones could trick your mind.

I tried to be smarter than the test, so I waited until the last possible moment to test rather than the first moment I knew I could test. I never had a false positive, so I would be pregnant if I saw the + sign. Up to this point I'd probably taken at least fifty pregnancy tests. At Surrogate Mothers Online, we called it "POAS" when we wrote online. It stood for "Pee-On-A-Stick." I swear it was an addiction unto itself, and even when you knew you were pregnant you'd test again just to see a darker line.

I waited, thinking I'm pretty sure I'm pregnant for Bev and Dave. The test came up positive +. I got an immediate surge and huge adrenaline rush throughout my body. I felt a sea of hormones pumping throughout my entire body and like I was full of life again. I jumped up and down, so happy that I could tell Bev I was pregnant.

Maddie, my past intended mother in my previous surrogacy, didn't want to know if I did a home pregnancy test, but Bev did. I called her to tell her the good news. She was so happy but of course hesitant. I had come to know the sound tone of that happy voice, the voice that says, "I just can't wait to have my child in my arms to believe it all."

Bev and Dave were very wary the first transfer would work because the embryo quality was not very good according to the doctor. The embryos were mixed; one was their own embryo and one was from a donor egg. They had their hopes up just like I did, they wanted to be parents.

Like so many couples they tried so many times before and had been to a geneticist. Bev was given no reason why she couldn't carry a baby. I felt huge compassion for women who heard or feared they might hear the words "You'll probably never carry a child." I couldn't imagine.

On January 26, 2006, after our first transfer and at our first appointment with a new fertility doctor and clinic, we heard one heartbeat. The look on Bev's face was precious, and Dave had the same look. Happiness was always the reward with expecting a baby, but in surrogacy it was always a surefooted tactic to save the pure and ultimate happiness for when they had their baby in their arms, in their home and their lives.

I knew that they had wanted twins because they didn't want to have to do surrogacy again. But, when you transfer embryos that aren't likely to make it, as in their case, there isn't much of a chance that two will survive the thaw let alone the implantation. Healthy embryos were the only ones that were going to make it. I probably would have done the exact thing they did with their embryos. The singleton heartbeat was strong, and we were pregnant! Bev and Dave were thrilled.

At this point, I've carried my own two boys, both singletons. My surrogacy history after my boys was a singleton, twins, twins, and now a singleton. For those who do the math, this was my sixth pregnancy and eighth baby.

I thought about how I could hide the pregnancy at work. A single pregnancy was a little bit easier to carry, and I wouldn't get as big as I did with twins but ultimately there was no way I was going to be able to hide it. I get big and round during pregnancy whether it's a singleton or twins. There were far fewer complications with a singleton, and I could wait as long as possible with big shirts to reveal I was pregnant. Again.

Before the transfer with Bev and Dave, I took a few days of vacation from work so the boys and I could move again. I found a house in the town right next to the one we had lived in for years so the boys could go to good schools.

I expected, and got, a hassle with the school district after I put an application in for the boys to attend their next year in high school. Luckily, a friend at work in our legal department told me about grandfather rules in schools. Because the boys had been grandfathered into the school system (having been there for over ten years) we should have a better chance of getting a transfer into their current school. The school district continued to fight me until I pulled the grandfather card. Thankfully, we were awarded the school permit needed for them to finish school at their current high school.

Terrie was still living in the apartment she moved to years ago, and we'd moved a handful of times, almost the same number as the number of surrogate journeys I'd had. It was so frustrating to move so often, but I wanted to keep the boys in the same school. I held out the hope that one day, one day I could find a place we wouldn't have to move from. Home was where we were, and where we'd always be together no matter what, but it was my golden dream to be able to buy a home, stay put, and not have to move again.

I started to think about my dreams. What was it that I wanted? I was giving people their dreams, but I wasn't giving myself one damn thing. I patted my tummy with

Bev and Dave's little one inside. I began hoping one day, at some point, I could make extra money and buy a house. But, as I was saving for the boys' college, if felt like the home might never happen.

I refused to give up on my dream, but there was never enough money to even think of buying a home. I cut coupons, worked harder, and I never got close to saving enough. I didn't squander money, and I bought things only on sale for the most part. I wondered if it would ever happen. I had no huge down payment because anything extra was going into the boys' college account. I was nowhere close to my dream but maybe that's why it was a dream, something to think about and hope for. It was way too expensive where we lived, but I still held onto that ridiculous far-fetched dream.

I remembered back to a school project I kept that Steven did back in first or second grade. It was about the important people in their lives, and what they hoped for and dreamed about. He wrote, "My mom is the most important person to me, and she dreams about living in a house." I'll never forget that. I posted it on the wall in my bedroom for years until I took it down when we had to move again.

The boys would be out of the house soon, though I wasn't ready, but I would do anything to make their dreams come true.

TEN

JOURNEY #4 BIRTH

The days, weeks, and months went by fast. I was 39½ weeks pregnant with Bev's and Dave's little boy. The almost new parents were beside themselves, simply overjoyed to have a son, and sent me beautiful, heartwarming cards every month, or they'd come over to see us any chance they got to rub my belly. It was these little things that meant a lot to me. I enjoyed every single minute of the pregnancy.

The day before our due date I decided to have pictures done. I went over to the local Glamour Shots to get a few photos before the birth of their little boy. We decided to let the pregnancy happen naturally and not plan a date. I sensed it was too early, and I felt especially beautiful and very pregnant that evening and wanted to cherish the memories.

I had a feeling that this little boy would be my last surrogacy. It was so bittersweet. It wasn't that I didn't want to be pregnant again, but I just had this sense I wouldn't be able to do it again, and he'd be my last baby. I'm sure it had a lot to do with my OBGYN, Dr. Kazman, and his opinion of my surrogacy history. I knew I was pushing the boundaries where he felt comfortable with approving another surrogacy. I would totally respect a medical opinion, not a personal one.

I ended up going back to him because Bev knew him through the medical grapevine. She respected his work, as did I, along with being his patient quite a few times. We agreed it'd be best to go back to the doctor we both knew and trusted. I didn't want to do anything that would jeopardize my health, and I trusted Dr. Kazman.

Maybe I was pushing things at work, at home, and with myself. It made me think about how doing surrogacy made me hide more in my life. It protected me in the dating world, and I tended to hide more at work because I never wanted to make a commotion with others. When I was visually pregnant at work people talked, and I hid more. I always had to explain myself. I was doing something that was out of the ordinary and it started to become uncomfortable for me. I started to hunger for more in my life, for more than being pregnant all the time.

When I was on Surrogate Mothers Online I would often see how women had great relationships while they were surrogates. I understood it was possible, but realized it couldn't be for me if I kept up this kind of life.

Most of the surrogates knew their husbands before they became surrogates. And most of the intended mothers looking for a surrogate had a supportive husband. Then there was me, a single surrogate mother.

Dr. Kazman had approved me to work up until my due date, which was the next day. I had several different outfits for my Glamour Shots pictures, and they provided a few drapes to use.

"I'd like to get a few shots of my pregnant belly."

"Okay sure," the young twenty-something male at the counter said. He was sipping on a cola when I walked in and seemed like an open-minded young man.

I spent about two hours with Jason, the photographer, and even went the extra mile doing some naked pictures with my belly. I'd never taken naked pictures before, but I was glad I did. It was all very discreet, and Jason was unbelievably professional.

I was huge, and Baby Boy was dropping. I could feel the baby moving down and my belly was slightly contracting while Jason was waiting for me to change. There was another pregnant woman behind me, and we nodded and smiled at each other as she took her place in line. My face felt like it was glowing, and everything was very sentimental knowing it was going to end very soon.

I didn't want it to end.

I used the bathroom at the studio. I was starting to feel exhausted after a long day and ready to go home and rest. I felt my bladder being squished by Baby Boy as he kicked and stretched.

All of a sudden I felt a tickle coming down my leg. It was a leak coming from between my legs as I was putting on my stretch pants. I stopped and took a long look. I wasn't peeing. 'Hello, it's your amniotic water,' the logical voice inside my head said. I got on the phone with Bev and Dave and said, "It's time to meet your little boy! My amniotic water is leaking."

"Oh my God," Bev said. "Oh my God!" she repeated. I softly laughed.

"You're going to be a momma, Momma. Bev, can you call Dr. Kazman's office and let him know?"

"Yes, okay… well yes, of course. Oh my God. Dave! It's time, it's time!"

I met Bev and Dave at the hospital. Their little boy was coming fast.

"It's time!" Dave said excitedly. "You're going to be a daddy!" Bev said to Dave. They helped me up onto the bed in labor and delivery. Water gushed onto the floor. Contractions started very soon after and came on hard, just as hard as I'd remembered.

"Don't push, Susan," Bev said. "We've got to get the doctor in here because we'll need a C-section," she added.

"I know… I know." God, how I wanted to push. "He is a big boy so I don't think he's coming that fast," I said huffing and puffing. "The timing so far for everything is really good," I added as I breathed in and out with a contraction.

I still had makeup on from the photo studio and mentioned to Bev and Dave I'd just come from Glamour Shots. I thought about the review of pictures with Jason. My belly was especially huge with my arms barely able to make their way around my whole belly. I saw a ripe, round belly. What I didn't know then was that the start of the birthing process was minutes away.

The labor would get really hard. I'd breathe in hard and it'd go back out hard. I started to dread the thought of the postpartum feelings, the sea of the lost. I didn't want it, but it would come whether I wanted it or not. The natural state of my body would return to regular womanhood quietly, slowly, back to balance, to normalcy in about a year. I'd recognize myself when I fit back into my regular clothes, and when my moods balanced out. It always took that long until I started to feel like my non-pregnant-self again.

I envisioned my naked, round pregnant belly bumps in my mind, and how I looked in the mirror. Boomer, our dog, put his little chin on my bump every night while I read in bed. He knew life was there. I felt it in the shower or quietly resting my hand on my belly. I brought my hands around from the side to the front with excitement of what life I'd bring to the world.

Were all of our lives predestined, written out and planned before we came to this world? Did we come here to learn in this life, or relearn lessons that we didn't learn the first time around? Sometimes I'd think, what happened here, what happened in my life? How was it possible to love pregnancy this much?

For me, it was love at first pregnancy.

I was brought back to reality when Baby Boy gave me the hardest contraction yet, and I think I lost my breath in the middle of it. I huffed and I puffed knowing that giving birth was the one thing men couldn't do, it was the one thing we women do exclusively, and it made me feel stronger.

Dr. Kazman walked into the room. "Hi you guys! Well, here we are again! Susan, let's get ready for a repeat C-section," Dr. Kazman said.

"Can I go natural, Dr. Kazman?" I said through a contraction. He knew I wanted a "v-bac," a natural birth after a C-section.

"No can do, Susan. With multiple births, the C-section that you had last time weakened your uterine wall. Upon pushing you could have an abruption or put the baby or you in danger. Do no harm," he said as he moved around the room preparing for surgery.

I felt tears rolling down the side of my face, dreading the C-section. I trusted him and knew it was the right thing to do. I did not look forward to the recovery.

With mom and dad looking on, Bev and Dave's little boy was born, 8 lbs., 12 oz. The new parents were beyond over the moon. I loved seeing their faces the moment their baby was born.

I could see Bev planning out the next year of her little boy's life. Dave was standing by, not quite knowing just how their lives would be forever changed. I knew. I watched the two of them holding their new son. They were both in love with how good life was to them. I saw love between them and the love they'd have as a family. Their little boy would give them the love and peace of a family. They would receive pieces of their lives they didn't know were missing. This life I brought forth would forever change the world even in a small way by just being.

I realized at that moment that maybe I wasn't going after the thing I craved the most: Real love.

If you'd asked me then about finding a partner, I believe I'd have told you I was ready to find the love of my life. I was trying by dating, but always came up empty and alone. I was a single mother to two boys, raising them by myself for almost ten years. Where was the potential partner in my life?

The truth was it was hard to find a partner and to put yourself out there again with the potential to be hurt. Everything I was doing was not moving me toward that goal. I kept meeting men who in my eyes were not available. That was a big word in my vocabulary lately, "availability."

Bev put her little boy into my arms after Dr. Kazman stitched me up. I held him close and whispered, "Welcome to the world, little one." I touched his sweet little head and gave him a kiss on his forehead then smelled it. "MMMMMmmmmm, baby smell," I said. "You are so wanted, so loved." I admired him more and recognized the weight of his body had lifted from mine.

"We wouldn't have him without you. Thank you," Bev said, looking on, watching us. "You're welcome. He's beautiful," I said lovingly.

I wasn't sure what the psychic said about me to Bev before we started this journey, but I was sure it didn't matter anymore. I'm sure the psychic probably thought she picked up on some trust issue, who knows? I certainly wasn't perfect and my personal life choices probably weren't the best, and God knows I've made a lot of mistakes. I've fallen a lot, but I've always gotten back up and shown up even if it was later.

One thing I knew that the psychic didn't know was that I knew what my body could do and that I would never intentionally hurt another human being.

ELEVEN

SOUL SCARS

What I called "the fourth trimester of pregnancy" came with a vengeance. It seriously felt like depression, again. It seemed each post-pregnancy was getting worse and worse in the way of a total hormone grand slam down.

This one was worse than previous ones. I didn't feel like I needed to see a therapist because I knew it'd be over in a few months. It was getting through those months that proved to be the hardest.

I kept trying to remember who I was. I always lost a little sense of self in the fourth trimester and some days were harder than others to deal with.

I was back at work six weeks after my second C-section. I dropped right back into my position, and our department was growing. Kevin had wrapped up the new training before I left on maternity leave, and we were heading in a whole new direction since the new performance process and the form for it was rolled out company-wide.

Kevin hired two new women, Diane and Julie, into our department. I got to know them briefly before I left for maternity leave. They were going to help us expand our department into the Organizational Development Department for the company. In the short time I spent with them, it seemed they were a great addition to our team. They were both PhDs, one of them with two PhDs. We had more people in our office than we had room. One office was added down the hall.

I was learning so much, but the hormone drag I was feeling postpartum was kicking my ass. I had trouble keeping any muscle memory and keeping up with new terms and all the new material. I was assisting Kevin and three others in the department, and had trouble just keeping up with Kevin. It was a tough adjustment, but I was working on it.

Although I was trying, I felt myself slipping in the ability to take care of three people. I would berate myself for not keeping up and get pissed off about it. I resented these huge changes and sometimes I wished things could stay the way they were. Kevin stepped in and lightened my load. He was a fair boss.

I tried my best to keep a low profile at work. I knew there were some people like Carol who didn't agree with surrogacy. She knew I was back, and the gossip was unrelenting. The only way I knew about it was that a few women would come to me and ask me if I knew she was spreading bad things about me.

The things she said were the same as before. "Susan is a womb for rent, just like Oprah said. Getting pregnant over and over again when there are needy children in the world who need to be adopted is just wrong, plain wrong," she said to every human ear she could find. She'd been at the company for a long time so she knew a lot of people. I simply ignored her as best I could.

It did make me hide more, and I was ridiculously good at it, and I continued to hide and make myself small often. In some ways it didn't make sense, because, typically, if you asked anyone close to me they would say that I loved the spotlight, and I did. I'm an extrovert. There were many reasons why I hid at work, but it was usually because I didn't feel I measured up to others. Polar opposites were clearly in my life.

I can trace some of this back to an early time in my life when my self-esteem started to crack, when I felt less than. There were many times I felt it, but I thought about a time when I was maybe ten or eleven.

The family, my stepfather, my mother, sister, brother, and I were watching a Miss America show. It was tense, down to the final countdown, who was going to win and get the crown? My mother was bombed, and so was my stepfather, Donald. My older brother might have been there, but I can't quite remember because usually he was in his room studying or out playing baseball.

I wanted desperately to be like the beautiful girls on television. They were gorgeous and what I thought was smart, and I wanted to be them. 'Maybe one day,' I thought. I'd parade around with my hairbrush to my mouth pretending I was the beautiful one singing in front of the mirror when no one was looking.

As the countdown began all of us started making a lot of noise about who we wanted to win. I think everyone wanted one woman, and I wanted the other. Whatever show or sport or movie it was it didn't matter because I would always root for the underdog.

My stepfather yelled at me, "Susan, get me a beer!" I ran as fast as lightning to the fridge to get a beer for him and got back just in time for the reveal of Miss America.

"The winner is…." and the announcer said my underdog's name. "I won! I mean she won!" I said. "My girl won!" My arms went straight up into the air. "Yay!" I yelled.

All of a sudden I felt something cold and wet coming down on my head, over my face, off my shoulders, and onto the front and back of my shirt and pants. It stunk and it was cold. I brought my arms down slowly as what I recognized to be beer was pouring down from my head, soaking and matting my hair. I was mortified. My stepfather poured the whole can of cold beer on my head and made me sit there until he was done pouring the can.

Then he screamed loudly at me, "Clean it up you little brat! You're a nothing!" I went numb and ran off to clean it up.

His voice was the scariest, meanest voice I've ever heard in my life. I can't remember hearing anything from him other than his yelling.

At night, my stepfather would come into the room I shared with my sister. While we were sleeping he would touch me inappropriately and take what wasn't his to take. In those moments, I'd go off somewhere, anywhere, in my mind to escape and not be present with that man.

This is the reality, the truth of what I lived with from five to thirteen years old. Being treated inhumanely, with malice and manipulation eats at your soul, it drowns your voice, who you are, and can make you hide with shame because you feel less than.

I was almost two months postpartum. I went in and out of the days, one by one waiting to feel better. It seemed like one day was just like another. Waking up, going to work, coming home, making dinner for the boys, going to bed, and starting it all over again.

When I felt less than low, so low I didn't think I could go lower, I sought out anything that made me feel somewhat comfortable, and, something that made me feel wanted and loved. That something I knew was no good for my life but would lend an ear to me, and just listen. Something that was secret in my life, to my family and friends. Something I thought would make me feel better even knowing it's only for a moment.

I called my married lover, Adam.

It had been over two years since I'd seen him, and when I called him it was like he had been waiting for my call. I still wanted him and thought I needed him.

I told myself it was just to say hello, but deep down I knew better than that and so did he. I knew all it would take is for him to reach out to kiss me. I resisted for two long years and I was so strong during that time. I felt like I had made progress then, but apparently I wasn't making enough.

I hadn't emailed him during that time because I knew I'd break and end up calling him. He was the only person I told almost everything to. I wondered why it was always when I was at my lowest point that I'd call him. So, I reached out when I finally felt I really needed someone.

Everything was secret about us, even the love between us, if love resided there at all. It was not talked about. I thought about it often. The only thing he really was to me was my confidant, my lover. He helped me hide and stay small, but he didn't know that, and at the time, neither did I.

After I called him and we said our hellos, we had that same silence on the phone like so many times before. Our silence said so much.

I didn't expect that he'd come over right away, but he came over in less than an hour after I called. We had decided to meet at my house during the day. He walked up the narrow pathway and up the steps to the house. I stood at the front door and looked at his new car in my driveway, a red Mustang.

Maybe he had changed during the time we didn't see each other. He had gone from a family van to a hot little car. I couldn't help but think about the old story of sports cars and the midlife men who drove them, screaming of a possible mid-life crisis. In the past he would have reached over to kiss me at the top of the stairs, but I backed up instead and let him in the house.

"Well, hello," he said and moved to kiss me in between the washer and dryer right by the door. "Hello," I said shyly.

The years were aging both of us. but it only took one kiss, deeply sensuous, the kind of kiss that takes you by surprise, but the kiss you know intimately and remember. He started to walk as we were kissing. I backed up as he moved, still kissing him.

One unending kiss and we were moving to my bedroom around the corner toward what we knew to be real for us. The passion between us felt so good, the rightness of being kissed and touched. I felt human again. The excitement was intense, addictive, and felt almost new for me because it'd been so long.

He didn't know that I'd had three more babies since I'd seen him. He didn't know where I was in my life, and I didn't know where he was in his life.

We kissed long and hard, soft and delicate. He pulled my dress off over my head, and then stood back looking at me. I pulled his red shirt off over his head and my hands touched the skin on his chest. I remembered. Our clothes were off in record time except for my black lacy panties. I kept kissing him wanting to delay taking my panties off in front of him. I was very secretive about my C-section scar. I sometimes pretended it wasn't there, but I knew it was. I cringed when I'd look at it. I hated it and felt self-conscious. It was still tender. He put two fingers in the hem of my panties, and slowly moved them down. I grabbed his arm and held it firm. "No, it's, um…"

"It's okay…" he said tenderly, "let me touch you." My head fell back and I felt my shame fall right away, down and out of my toes. I gulped air as he pulled my panties down slowly, inch by inch. Half way down he sighed when he saw my scar. He kissed it gently, softly. I sighed the deepest, longest sigh I'd ever experienced.

A tear came down my cheek. I wiped it away. He looked up at me, and whispered, "You're still beautiful inside and out."

I've never felt more seen and accepted in my life. It touched me that he could feel so deeply. I suddenly saw the part of him that I remembered, adored, and loved. His smile brought back the best of times.

I fell deeper. That day was probably one of the very few times we actually made love. I knew it was love from the way we connected as one. Most all of the other times were about sex and our primal human needs.

Sometimes I wished we'd never made love because I would hold onto it desperately, like it would never come around again, that hope of love, that hope for more. I did want more. I was starting to want to settle down with someone special and share my life.

I told Adam about the whole Oprah incident. He never followed Oprah, so he didn't know about it. He was amazed. I told him about my total disappointment about the "womb for rent" label and how upset I was about it.

"Susan, you have a wild streak wider than the sky, and a free spirit that goes on forever. I can't believe you'd let a label to sell magazines get you down." He stroked my back and looked into my eyes. "But, Oprah," I said and looked back into his eyes.

"Doesn't matter. You're a non-conformist," he said with total confidence. "Plus, I believe you told me one time that labels don't suit you. And to never label you with anything."

He reached over and stroked my legs up and down lightly. I did say that, and I've said that to other people many times. Why couldn't I put this with other old memories and keep it there for good, or just let it go?

After Adam left, I remembered reading somewhere that there is no such thing as life with no pain. Simultaneously I looked over at my dresser and noticed an old, tattered piece of orange colored paper, a Post-It with an affirmation I'd put on the mirror that read, "Pain is Certain, Suffering Is Optional." I hadn't read it for a while and actually forgot it was there.

It is?

Is suffering optional?

How do I get there?

I pondered my tender C-section scar, the one I will have for life for bringing life out of my body and into the world. Maybe those physical scars are our war wounds to remind us of our healing, that we survived whatever it was we went through.

I still had what I called "soul scars" deep inside that I wouldn't bring out for years. As I thought about Adam kissing my scar, I wished for a moment he could kiss those hidden scars, the ones I didn't tell even him about. The ones buried deep in my psyche, even ones from when I was a little girl. Soul scars were place to put these feelings, like a Pandora's box. The one only I visit, the place of the invisible scars you can't see with the naked eye, nor let others ever see.

The raw one there was the reduction (selective abortion) from triplets to twins during my second journey. I was pregnant with three fetuses, which were reduced, in utero to two. It was the one soul scar I never talked about to anyone.

I could feel the indelibly branded scar upon my soul, deep inside. It'd rear its ugly head sometimes when I felt less than. It was thick and gnarly looking and hung like a big storm cloud, weighing heavily on my body. It fogged my mind and pierced my heart. It still hurt like a gaping, open wound, one that wouldn't heal no matter how much I tried to close it.

I didn't want to feel it. Soul scars are worse than physical scars because you can't see them. I mostly chose to not look. It hurt too much. But I carried it day after day, safely tucked into my consciousness and knowingness because it wasn't safe yet to deal with.

I willed the soul scar to stop bleeding, to let me live, but it wouldn't until I was ready to look at it head on and humbly acknowledge its existence, that it was part of who I was, as a human, and part of what made me the woman I was to this point in my life.

I tenderly bandaged it again with denial and told myself to get over it for now. I made the choice to carry it longer because it wasn't safe yet to share.

TWELVE

UNFOLDING

Six months after my fourth surrogate journey I woke up one February morning feeling like myself again. I finally felt I was getting back into the grove of my own life. It's funny how this happens.

Things at work were going well, and I was getting to know our new employees, Diane and Julie. I was working closely with Kevin to finish up some research that led to a lot more research for many projects we were working on in our department. Kevin had implemented the new performance system in the company, with my assistance, and we were moving on to new, exciting human development changes for our HR department.

Our new group and new employees were delving deep into adult development, also called Integral Studies. There are many books written with explanations of what Integral Studies are, and, to be clear, I'm sharing my personal experience with it, and my own opinions about it.

The development part is that, in general, human beings go through a series of stages of development throughout their entire lifetime, from infancy to being an elder adult. Some continue to grow and learn more about the world around them after the youth and young adult growth stages are complete, and move 'up' into the upper stages seeking to become even more comprehensively integrated, to learn more deeply of the latter stages of adult development.

When I first heard about adult development, I thought, 'What? How could this be that no one ever told me anything about this?' I was forty-seven at the time. I only thought there was college after high school, not a huge, expansive world of adult development. I was innately curious and hungry to learn more about why I am who I am, and my place in the world.

Integral thinking and integral practice move into the later stages of adult development. For me, after I started learning things about myself, it started to fall into place. 'Uni-verse,' one world, started to make sense to me, and understanding this leads to greater understanding within ourselves. The practice involved in Integral Studies itself goes back thousands of years, but it was new to our company.

As part of Human Resources, we were opening up to new developments and opportunities with organizational development. I initially didn't realize how it would affect me on a personal level.

From the moment I began to open up to Integral Studies, it felt as if my life was on a new trajectory. I felt like a thirsty sponge ready to soak up everything my mind and soul could learn. A lot of it was way over my head, but I just kept moving forward, staying open, and learning more. What I loved most about it was that I was always learning something new about myself. It was exciting, and provided a different way to see myself, and my whole life, more clearly. And it was my work, I was doing this research every single day.

I'd always been hungry for knowledge, to learn and understand things I didn't know about. I spent hours every day on the computer doing research for Kevin. I had approval to look through anything, literally anything available through our company world-wide library system to do further research into Integral Studies.

The virtual library was a knowledge smorgasbord for me, and I was hungry. I found anything and everything I could ever need once I knew where to look. One article referred to another article, then to a book, and so on until I had so much information that we would never be able to read all the materials.

Kevin was focusing on leadership for the company to help our managers become more independent thinkers with their managerial style. Sometimes I'd have four different librarians looking for various pieces of information Kevin requested.

Within our new performance system, there was a part of the review form that Kevin formulated into it a requirement for the employee to choose at least one thing they had to be working on, something to improve about themselves.

Not everyone liked this new part because they thought that they were perfect just the way they were, but it was now required to work on self-growth in one way of their choosing which was then approved by their manager. This new form and process didn't make us popular with the rest of the company.

We were doing new things and promoting change, and that — change — was something a lot of the company was uncomfortable with. I found there were hundreds of books written on that topic alone.

I, for one, was grateful because I'd never been in a company where they gave a damn about employees, let alone pay for something to help their employees grow and improve their work and personal lives. We had every convenient thing at work, a cafeteria, a gym, a library, everything one would need. Now employees had a growth opportunity.

Kevin gave me daily book orders for our department. I'd put orders into the library and for months we'd receive books, sometimes on a daily basis. It was like Christmas time for me.

The first few books we received were, The Art of Waking People Up by Cloke and Goldsmith, and Immunity To Change by Kegan and Lahey. The second book about change would be a portal to my first transformation.

We also had articles coming via email as we were preparing for our first workshop training for managers. What I didn't know at this early stage was that before I could even entertain the thought of my reality changing, I'd have to face a lot of hard truths.

The topics we were collecting were diverse, from increasing awareness, courageous listening, meditation, and problem solving to conflict resolution and many more. It was company oriented with leadership in mind, but there were always nuggets that applied to more than that, and takeaways that you could use for yourself. It was so interesting. These weren't books you read to be entertained. They had challenging personal tests to work through and complete. There were a lot of things I could change about myself, but had no idea where to start, so I just kept reading and trying to understand it all.

February, 2007

A few days after Valentine's Day I received a call from Maddie and Ben. It happened to be the twins third birthday that week and they were driving to upstate New York to celebrate with family and relatives. I remembered my surrogate babies' birthdays; it was almost like remembering my own kids' birthdays, yet so different since I wasn't living with my surrogate babies.

I was sitting in my bedroom on my bed talking to Maddie on the phone. She was such a proud mama and she was telling me all about the twins' lives and their different personalities, what they were learning, and what types of books she read to them at night before they go to bed.

"Tank you fer my birfday," I heard one of the twins say to me, then two little voices laughing and giggling, fighting over the phone. "Me, me, mine!"

"That was Jake," Maddie said. "They are growing up so fast, Susan!"

"Momma, mine!" I heard one of them say.

Jake thanking me for his birthday was over the top while they were little and the sweetest thing anyone had ever said to me.

"Ben and I made an agreement," Maddie announced.

"The agreement is that we would give you some information and then bow out as soon as we give it to you. It doesn't matter whether you say yes or no, it won't change how we feel about you. This information is for you only."

My curiosity was immediately piqued.

"Remember the guy that came to visit you in the hospital three years ago right after the birth of the twins?" Maddie asked.

"Yeah, I remember that guy," I said. I threw my legs and bare feet up on the wall to stretch after my earlier workout. It was a guy Maddie knew who was handsome, interesting, and very personable. I had told Maddie later he was someone I would definitely date.

"He's gay!" she said as she smiled, almost laughing. Maddie got a kick out of my "terrible gay-dar," as she used to say.

"Oh!" I had exclaimed. I was always that way about people who are gay. I didn't really notice or know who was gay or not as it didn't matter to me. I didn't pay any attention to it unless the people somehow made it obvious they were a same-sex couple. And even then sometimes I didn't take notice or think much about it.

"Anyway," she said, as the twins were babbling in the background, "he has two male friends who are gay and living together as a couple, and they are also very good friends of mine and Ben's. I went to college with one of them and they've been together now as a couple for about sixteen years. They are looking to build a family and would like to know if you'd be interested in being a surrogate mother for them. I promised them I'd tell you about them but I also made an agreement with Ben that it would be all we'd say about the subject. It's totally up to you because we didn't know where you would be with surrogacy or being a surrogate again."

"Wow, really? Okay..." I said to Maddie. "I'm always open to knowing people who know people. I'll think about it," I added. I brought my feet down from the wall and stretched them out.

"Ross and Martin would love to just come and meet you to see if maybe you would all get along, to see if there is any chemistry in working together, and they'd meet you whenever you're ready," Maddie said.

The truth was, I had already been thinking about doing surrogacy one more time. 'One more time' was getting old,' I thought to myself, and I was a little unsettled because I knew my mother would have a fit. I knew I wanted to do another independent journey without an agency because I had done it with Bev and Dave, and it turned out well. It was almost impossible to find a couple via any other route for surrogacy and I did not want to go through getting an agency.

'A gay couple,' I thought. I got up for a shower and couldn't get my mind off of my next potential journey. Wow. I'd never really thought about helping a gay couple before. I wasn't really sure where I stood in doing so because it had never been presented for me to consider.

I had many surrogate friends who would only carry for gay couples.

"It's way less drama than with couples with infertility issues. It's just the guys and me," some of my surrogate friends said.

A few years ago I was approached by Lauren and Tracey, from my former agency, to do an anonymous journey for a nameless celebrity. Although the deal was lucrative and tempting, I couldn't see doing a journey with no waiting parents, no one to get to know and get excited with. The deal was I could never meet the intended parents or parent. I ultimately said no because I wanted to know who I was doing surrogacy for. The deal didn't go through, but I felt good about turning it down.

Like any potential surrogacy couple, what mattered most for me was what kind of people they were. I couldn't care less what their sexual preference was. I was getting better at trusting my intuition. This time it told me to go ahead and check them out, get to know them first like I would with any other couple.

I knew Maddie and Ben wouldn't send me anyone that they themselves didn't trust. Martin and Ross had been together a long time and their relationship was established.

The couple, Ross and Martin, and I shared emails and phone calls back and forth for a good month before they came to my house to meet me, Brian, and Steven. The first picture they sent me of themselves was a picture of them both in a little dinghy on the ocean in what looked like Mexico. My first thought was, 'It's not fair. They look like amazing men. I can't believe they are gay.' I secretly wished they weren't gay. Of course, I knew this was silly but couldn't help thinking they looked like the type of men I would love to know, to date, and to marry. I couldn't help but think for the millionth time that all the good ones were taken.

I have a few friends who are gay but most of them are out of state. In my experience, there is something special about the way gay people are themselves, just so real. I believe when they come out with who they really are they are relieved to simply be authentic. They don't live like those who pretend they are one thing when they really are another.

In the second email, Martin sent a picture of the both of them with their dog. "We are a lot alike, and here is our dog, Buster." It didn't take long: I was in love. Ross and Martin were versions of light and dark twins. They didn't look exactly alike but were alike in a lot of ways. I mostly talked with Martin via email.

They sounded like a wonderful couple. They were excited to start a family after so many years together. They seemed a lot like Maddie and Ben, easygoing and straight-forward, and very private.

Eventually they came over to my house to meet me, and my sons. I explained to the boys that these intended parents were gay. They were immediately open to it and that surprised me in a lot of ways. We were all opening up in new ways, I realized.

I met Ross and Martin at our house one late afternoon when they had a business trip that brought them to Los Angeles. They lived in New Jersey and stayed for a brief visit. From what I could tell by meeting them in person, they were exactly who they said they were, or who I could know as intended parents. Ross worked for a family business and Martin had his own advertising company.

We made the usual small talk, and one comment Martin made stuck in my mind.

"I can't wait to have our own child. I'd quit working or sell my business to spend time with our child." He was already planning to spend time with his unborn children!

Brian and Steven were there, and I could tell they liked Ross and Martin, too. Even though I had only known them for a very short time, it felt right to be their surrogate, just like it did with Maddie and Ben. There is something about working with people on a surrogate journey who personally knows someone I know. I can't say for sure what it is exactly, but trust comes to mind. It helped me trust them more. Trust had been a word I wasn't always comfortable with.

The next afternoon after work I got an unexpected call, a call from Bev and Dave.

"Are you ready to move to our next journey?" Dave asked.

I said nothing, wondering what he meant: I didn't remember them asking me if I'd do another journey. I do remember them saying something about another journey but that was right after I gave birth, and we never talked about it again. I had attended their little boy's christening a few months after he was born, and they were so very happy, but we didn't talk about it then, either. I had no real idea they were ready to move ahead with a sibling for their son.

"Susan?" Dave said.

"Um, another journey?" I asked, holding my cell phone closely. I'd left my desk at work and walked outside so I could talk openly with Dave.

I suddenly had flashbacks to my first two journeys when the intended parents asked me if I could be a surrogate for them again. A flight or fight feeling came up. I felt uneasy. I didn't want to disappoint anyone, but I wasn't going to move forward with a second journey, and I didn't know what to tell Dave except for the truth.

I explained what I could, and said, "We can't move forward with another journey. I've already committed myself to another couple ready to move forward." And with that, it was over.

I felt terrible about not taking them seriously when they mentioned it way back when, but they never followed up on it. There was nothing I could do to change it now.

THIRTEEN

JOURNEY #5 START

I had been trying to date and was putting myself out there, but I wasn't receiving much back. In one situation, I went to lunch for a first date, set up through It's Just Lunch again, and the date left me reeling. The man didn't do anything wrong, and, in fact, he was nice, but it just felt like he wasn't my type.

As I sat there, I explored why he wasn't my type and tried to figure out what triggered me so strongly about him. I thought I'd dealt with a lot of this relational stuff a long time ago.

I didn't even give myself a moment to get to know him. Instead, I just quickly created a list of things that wouldn't work for me. It woke up some deep-rooted insecurity inside, and they were things I knew to be my problems. Clearly, I wasn't ready. I had visions of looking in the mirror at myself and asking 'why? Why isn't this working, Susan?'

Although, there was this: He talked about his ex-wife.

"You look just like my ex-wife. Truly, the resemblance is amazing," he said, looking deeply into my eyes within five minutes of meeting me. Yep, that was it. I could just imagine myself in bed with him, hearing him either say it again or mistake me for his ex-wife.

I smiled and nodded, thinking 'oh my God, really? Did he just say I looked like his ex-wife? Why in the world would he want to be with someone who reminded him of his ex? Why would he say that to me? Why were we even talking about his ex?'

I accepted a second date invitation from him knowing I shouldn't. I think I was surprised I actually got a second date and guessed that he sensed my desperateness with dating. Obviously, we both had a lot to work on.

I wasn't getting very many dates on It's Just Lunch because of the unfavorable male to female ratio, and, I swear to God, the men dating all of us women knew we didn't have much choice. I had just started the dating scene and already wanted to leave it again. 'Pregnancy would take me out of it again,' I thought.

The second date didn't turn out well either, not surprisingly, and when I turned down a third, my reaction to the invite showed me where I was at in my life: I wasn't in a good place for a new relationship.

Over the next few months, Martin, Ross and I worked on agreements for our surrogacy arrangement. We would be doing the egg transfer soon after all the paperwork was done.

It seemed kind of pointless to try to bring in a new man into my life, but I kept hoping there would be a man that might understand. It felt rather hopeless because I would have to say something like, "Oh, hey, hi. You seem like a really nice guy. Do you mind that I'll be pregnant soon for a gay couple while we are getting to know each other?"

Yep, it was pointless. That, and all I was meeting were men who were not a good match in some form or another. I put dating on the back burner.

I threw myself into surrogacy again, this time journeying with Ross and Martin. I was really excited to be working with them because they seemed like such great people. They were both self-sufficient and working for themselves.

I was open to a new couple and hopefully some new friends. You never know how a surrogacy will work. I always hoped all of my intended parents would stay friends and yet I certainly learned not to expect anything.

I knew the ropes well enough now to be able to look ahead at what would be expected in way of contracts, medical appointments, and everything else. I definitely didn't need hand-holding. We discussed agencies, but far as I understood, we wouldn't need one.

We arranged for a date to meet so we could go over some items on the contract. As we were talking over lunch at a quaint little Italian place, I could see that Ross and Martin were preparing to become dads.

"I've never seen Maddie so happy," Ross said. "I mean, she's a different person as a mother." He sipped his water and told me all about their college days.

"I think she was meant to be a mother. And Ben a father, too, it's really amazing how dreams come true. They waited so long."

That made me so happy. I absolutely loved hearing about the family I helped grow. It was wonderful to hear comments from someone on the outside looking in.

As we continued talking, Ross and Martin gave me an open window into their lives, how they imagined parenthood to be, and what their plans were for the first year or so.

"We've always wanted children," Martin said, smiling from ear to ear. I thought to myself what great parents they would make.

As we discussed the agreement, the agency came up. "We don't need to use an agency," I said. "It will save you both a lot of money."

"No, really, Susan. It's fine. I'd like them to handle all the financials instead of us doing it ourselves. The third party, the agency, will handle the contracts, financials, etc., cross the t's, dot the i's so we can enjoy our journey," Martin said.

I was surprised, but it made sense to me. I was so programmed to save money, not just for myself but for others. I certainly didn't make a lot of money being a surrogate mother, but it definitely helped out our family.

"Okay," I said, though with some hesitancy. I then imagined how nice it would be not to bring up the business side of surrogacy and just move along with our journey. As the afternoon went on, it made more sense to me to just let it be. I knew of the agency they wanted to use. It was the best and the longest standing surrogacy agency there was in Los Angeles.

I knew they would request a lot of things up front and a few things they might challenge me on, but I also knew we would be in good hands with them. Ross and Martin made it clear they were not going to worry about the costs. They wanted a family and needed help growing one.

We talked about everything, from kids, my sons, to dogs, to family, and much more. They were charming, friendly, and I really bonded with them well like I did with Maddie and Ben. I started picturing them as parents, seeing them holding their babies.

I often had visions in my mind, looking into the future and seeing things vividly. I always thought everyone had that ability, not seeing the future but visualizing it. One time when I told a friend I did that, she said, "Not everyone thinks like you do, Susan." I was honestly surprised. I found great value in my ability envision future things.

I had already Googled them both to find out as much as I could back before I met them. Ross was an important part of his family business, a huge global company that started some fifty-plus years before. Martin had his own start-up business, a very successful one.

After we discussed everything and we were ready to move ahead, the agency contacted me to get all the particulars on me, including my prior legal case with surrogacy. I told them my story of years ago, when the intended parents left me and the twins at the hospital, and how and why I took the babies home with me.

The agency requested a letter from Dr. Kazman clearing me for another surrogacy. They also requested many things a typical agency didn't ask for in way of private information including speaking to their psychologist. It was a big agency and they certainly knew how to conduct surrogacy journeys.

I looked forward to the phone call from the psychologist. It ended up being an interesting call because I spoke up and requested more information on the psychology of surrogacy. The psychologist sent me several articles about it. In the future, I had a desire to pursue this information about surrogacy. Why do we become surrogates? Why do we want to use our bodies to help someone else? There were so many whys but it all came down to choice of the woman.

I was invited into the agency to meet and visit with several staff there. One particular woman, who had been there for twenty years, told me they had one case where a very similar thing happened and it around the same time as my case. A woman who held a senior position went on to tell me that they took care of the problem swiftly.

"We nipped it in the bud before anything could happen. This couple simply changed their minds about wanting the children they created. It was a shock to us all that they would do such a thing, but they were filthy rich and complied with all the attorneys' requests," she said. I was listening intently.

"Then they signed away their rights so another couple could adopt the baby the day it was born," she explained. She seemed quite satisfied with what she was saying, speaking very matter-of-factly.

I nodded to let her know I was listening. I found it interesting, and quite frankly, that would have appealed to me greatly instead of all the drama I went through with taking the babies home with me in my second surrogacy journey.

"It all worked out because we did it the right way," she said. I had a slight pang, knowing it would have been so much better to have a good, competent agency working for me way back then. "They never had a disruption with the journey and the agency found parents to adopt the baby the day it was born," she stated.

I was learning so many things with this agency. I was invited to share at a weekly surrogate-get-together and decided to try it once because I was curious. I didn't have any intention of going weekly, though, because the agency was too far away and traffic in LA is almost always gruesome at the time it was held.

A few months later, after we jumped through all the necessary hoops, they hired one of the best clinics in southern

California and we were ready to move on. The reproductive endocrinologist was a doctor I hadn't worked with but I'd read all about his work. He was amazing and did infertility procedures others did not do. His statistics for success were the best around.

Every time I had an appointment or had to get something done the clinic was right on top of it. They were so wonderfully professional. Sometimes I was even able to do things over the phone or get a lab test close to my house. I never had to wait, and even though the drive was long, it was worth it because they were that good. There was only one doctor, Dr. Callahan, and the clinic was his private practice. He had one nurse, one receptionist, and an on-call embryologist. We had pleasant small talk each time I visited, and I felt comfortable with each item that had to be done to prepare for the journey.

We were nearly ready for the embryo transfer

Two weeks before the transfer and the egg donor was cycling, I was at the office getting a lining check. During the appointment Dr. Callahan called Ross and Martin and talked to them about their baby options. They decided they would try for twins.

"We talked about twins, so if you still want two, I would suggest taking sperm from each of you, keeping it separate petri dishes, and then using the same egg donor."

"That'd be great," Ross said. "Yes, that works," I heard him say on the phone without hesitation.

"I really like that idea, too," Martin added. I sat on the exam table amazed they could do such a thing. It seemed simple enough: if both embryos took, they both would be biological fathers to babies I would carry, and the babies would share a mother via egg donation. If only one made it they wouldn't know which embryo made it, and which one didn't, unless they did DNA tests (or unless, I suppose, some physical characteristic made it so obvious). Then they would cryopreserve the rest of the embryos.

The two weeks passed fast. I was lying on the exam table prepped for the embryo transfer waiting for the doctor. The embryologist walked into the exam room.

"It's complete, and so far all of the embryos successfully survived, and we have two beautiful embryos waiting to be implanted into their surrogate mother," he said. I smiled at the thought of being able to make a home for them for nine months.

"Wonderful! Can I see them?"

"Sure. One is a boy and one is a girl," the embryologist said. "I'll make sure you've done everything on our checklist, check identity again, and we'll move ahead with the transfer."

Apparently, all of the embryos that came back were girls except one. The clinic did testing on all of the embryos to give the parents the best and healthiest embryos. Ross and Martin didn't care about the gender and left it to the doctor to decide. At this point in time, this kind of procedure wasn't done often. The mixing of sperm with gay fathers was just becoming a thing. It took extra work on behalf of the embryologist.

My favorite part of surrogacy was looking at the embryos under the microscope, besides, of course, seeing the faces of the intended parents when the baby or babies were born.

I peered in to the microscope and viewed two beautiful round spheres developing before my eyes.

"I'll never get tired of seeing this," I said.

"Me, too, that's why I do what I do," he said.

The whole thing went like clockwork. We did the transfer in his office and then it was done. It was free of drama and went really well. Ross and Martin didn't make it for the transfer, but they were available via telephone while the transfer was being done. They were so excited!

"No going back now," Ross said on the phone. 'That's for sure!' I thought.

Ross and Martin arranged for care after the transfer for me. Well, they didn't themselves, but the agency did. They had a car to pick me up from the doctor's office and take me to a hotel where I'd rest for the next 48 hours. I had lots of books to read, and I was in heaven that I had time to myself. Two days was the doctor's protocol for the required time I was to stay off my feet. Some doctors required one day, some not at all, and others required two days. It was worked out to do the transfer on a Friday, I had Saturday and Sunday to rest, and then back to work on Monday.

With all the time on my hands, I started to think about work. I wondered if Kevin was getting tired of the whole pregnancy thing. The pregnancy did sometimes get in the way of work. It wasn't like they would do or say anything about my surrogacy, but I worried about it anyway. Kevin had always been supportive, but our department was growing, and I was very busy. I rationalized it thinking that if they were my own it wouldn't matter. But they weren't.

When I left the hotel on Sunday, I knew I was pregnant.

I just knew.

I wasn't going to share what I thought or my pregnancy testing until the guys wanted to know. The intended parents always want to know but don't believe you until they see the actual confirmation from the doctor. Only then does it start to sink in they are going to be parents.

I felt excited for Ross and Martin, but I was starting to lose some excitement of being pregnant: It was the first time I started to feel old being a surrogate mother. I think I was starting to put surrogacy behind me but decided to enjoy this last pregnancy and be present for all of it as much as I could.

I got home and the boys were off doing their own thing. One was at a friend's house and the other planning for college. Brian was a senior getting ready to go to Cal State Long Beach. I could tell Brian was excited to get out of the house and on his own, and remembered feeling that way when I was his age.

Ross and Martin both called me a few days later, and I told them I tested positive on the home pregnancy tests.

"Do you think it's twins?" Ross asked excitedly.

"I do, but I can't be completely sure, of course. My body feels very pregnant," I said excitedly.

A few weeks later a pregnancy blood test confirmed I was pregnant. The guys wanted to come out for the first ultrasound appointment. I met them at the doctor's office to learn how many babies we were pregnant with.

Ross and Martin stayed out of the office until we were all prepared and the ultrasound wand was already inside of me. Dr. Callahan had carefully prepared the vaginal ultrasound and then searched around with the wand, stopping every once in a while to measure.

"Okay," he said, "let's get going and see what we have."

"I know it's twins," I said. "I'm eating a lot more than usual and it feels like more than twins, like when I was pregnant with triplets, but I know that's impossible because we only put in two embryos," I added excitedly.

"Here is one… and yes, here is number two," Dr. Callahan said. He moved the ultrasound around, and then softly said, "We have another one."

"What?!" I said, shocked. "Wait. Three?" Martin and Ross looked at each other, then looked at me in surprise.

Ross and Martin were so excited, anticipating that both of the embryos made it, but no one expected three!

It was quiet. No one said a thing.

"Okay, you guys, don't get too worried. What we have here is that one of the embryos has split. It is quite common with IVF. Most of the time the third one will stop growing and the pregnancy will go back to twins, but we won't know for sure until the next ultrasound."

We were all happy yet shocked, staring at the screen in disbelief. One had Ross's sperm and the other had Martin's sperm, and one of them split into two. They were as surprised as I was. Dr. Callahan measured everything, making sure it was all growing according to schedule.

I was scared stiff.

I'd been pregnant with triplets before and it didn't turn out well. I started to fear the embryo would stay, yet I prayed it would go away naturally.

Martin started talking nervously about the nursery they were planning. Ross was still shocked and was just blankly staring.

"But, you only put in two, right?" I asked Dr. Callahan, feeling scared and confused like I did years ago, and still trying to understand what he had said. I was shocked. Desperate. Shocked, and feeling like I wanted confirmation that they'd take all three babies if there were three.

"This happens sometimes, Susan. There is always risk associated with multiples. There are even more rare times both embryos split and become quadruplets. It's still really early so don't worry. I predict the third will fizzle out before the twelve-week mark."

I was still scared.

I looked over at the guys wanting to say, I'll carry them all, please know, but I couldn't find my voice. We all walked out of the office together. Martin was as white as a ghost. Ross told me, "Don't worry Susan, it'll work out. We don't want you to be stressed." I didn't know what to say. We hugged, they touched my belly, comforting me with their hands and words, and we went our separate ways.

On the drive home I simply couldn't believe we had three hearts out of two embryos. I was forty-seven years old, wondering how the hell did I get myself into this mess again? I had promised myself I would not get into this kind of situation again.

But I did.

FOURTEEN

QUESTIONS
AND ANSWERS

That evening I picked up the phone to call my mother. "Mom, I'm pregnant with three," I said. I wasn't sure what I expected her to say but I knew she'd be there for me no matter what. Our relationship as mother and daughter was what I'd always wanted it to be: open and honest. I could tell her anything. She knew me better than anyone.

"What?!" she said. That 'what' was infamous to me. I could hear it anywhere, anytime, and knew it was hers, and hers alone. "What?!" the way my mom said it was always in the same tone.

I told her what the doctor said, and her only reply was, "Good God, let's hope it fizzles into the great unknown like the doctor said it would." I hoped that, too. Honestly, I did, and I thought about it every minute of the day.

"Mom, it's so good we can talk together. Thank you for always being there for me."

"Of course, honey, always," she said.

I thought about how different we both were. I loved to do a lot of things outside like planting, gardening, and fixing things up around the house, a DIY kind of girl. My mom liked those things, too, but she loved sewing, crocheting, knitting, and creating things with her hands. I would have an idea, like placemats for the kids, and she'd make it. I couldn't stand any of that and never learned it. I hated sewing and anything to do with yarn or crocheting. She was a whiz. All of her jobs were at retail stores with crafts and fabric and yarn. She made my clothes when I was a little girl. I hated every piece she made. We never agreed on clothes.

I thought about how we could not have more been more unalike. She had big feet. I had little feet. She had no boobs. I had big boobs. She always wondered where I got mine. She swears it was Grandma. She loved watching Letterman and the news. I didn't like watching television at all. It was depressing.

Despite our differences, I saw a lot of my mother in me and we'd always find common ground as mother and daughter. We were both tall and loved the beach, and most importantly we both loved being a mother. I always felt comfortable around her.

She said many things to me while I was growing up. Some of the things were really heated when she was mad at me. One of them was, "I hope you have a daughter just like you, so you could see what it's like to parent you! I wish that on you!"

I'd be a smart mouth and say, "I hope so, too, I'd love that!" I ended up having two boys before I divorced my ex-husband. I didn't think I'd have any more kids, especially after this last, fifth surrogacy.

"Do you have an extra few minutes to talk, Mom?" I said, knowing Letterman was coming on soon. She never missed a show.

"I'm always here for you to talk to."

"Remember I told you about the married man, the pastor I was sleeping with, my lover?

"Yes," she said softly.

"I want to stop loving him, but I don't know how," I whispered.

"Oh, honey," she said like only she could, "when the time is right, it will happen."

"I know it's not going anywhere, and it never will, but for some reason I can't stop loving him. It makes me crazy. I will myself to stop and I don't. It's been years, Mom."

"I know. It will happen, Susan."

For some reason I believed her. But I wanted it to stop, now.

After we hung up, I thought about my relationship with Adam. It always felt like I loved too much. I knew it was toxic. I thought of telling Adam's wife about our affair, but that would hurt her deeply and I didn't want to hurt her. But I desperately wanted to end our affair, and if I told her - it would end for sure. Forever. But the consequences of that would break up their marriage, their family, and maybe the church. I thought about the hurt that would radiate through their family. The two kids would be devastated, and he'd be kicked out as pastor at the church that he'd led for over twenty years. But, I would be done with him.

Still, it wasn't his wife's fault. I couldn't do that to her. I knew how it felt.

Adam must have sensed what I had been feeling because he called me that day to see how I was. I honestly was beside myself, stressed to the max. I had already told him what was going on with the pregnancy, and I had an appointment the next day to see if the third fetus was still there.

"How about we go away for a night?" Adam said. I got excited at that thought. I felt like I needed to get away. We only went away a handful of times in all our time together.

"Okay," I said. "That sounds nice." And, 'here we go again,' I thought. Dammit.

"It'll be a special place. Somewhere that is just ours," he said.

There was nothing I wanted more. Some place that only we would go, some place special, just for us.

The follow up appointment with Dr. Callahan was on a holiday, so I didn't have to go into work that day. I loved how things worked out sometimes. It would make the long drive somewhat enjoyable for check-in at the fertility clinic. Going south, it was a beautiful drive along the coast.

Ross and Martin met me late morning at Dr. Callahan's office. "We had an amazing brunch today at this little bed and breakfast down the way," Martin said.

"That's great," I said, and I could feel my stomach rumbling with coming hunger. I was always hungry when I was pregnant.

Everything was set up for the exam, and these exams had become so easy for me. I knew what to expect and assumed the position so we could take a view inside my uterus.

"Twins!" Dr. Callahan exclaimed, as he peered inside. "The other one fizzled out as predicted." I felt huge relief, and smiles were back on the guys' faces and mine. It was the best visit ever.

"Two little ones!" I said, relieved. I let out a big sigh. I could breathe again.

"We're so excited. When is the due date, doctor?"

"Let's see…" Dr. Callahan said. "Mid-April-ish," he said. "We'll get a more exact date as we move along. Susan will be with us here for twelve weeks and then she can move on to her OBGYN," he said.

To say I was relieved was an understatement: I was so fucking happy. I called my mom first when I got out of the appointment to let her know. I believe I told her those exact words. "Oh, thank God, honey!" my mom exclaimed.

"The guys" was how I referred to Ross and Martin when I talked to other people. I didn't tell everyone, of course. I did tell Adam a few weeks ago I was pregnant again, for a gay couple.

"Only you would do such a thing…" he said, hesitated, and then added, "help men have babies."

I wasn't sure how take that comment. To me it was a compliment because I was making a family. Who cares if it's for a man and a woman? Or a woman and a woman, a man and a man, or even a single person having a baby? I wasn't sure of his beliefs, or maybe he just didn't think God supported gay people. I wasn't going there.

"If men were supposed to have babies, they would be able to get pregnant," he said.

"Jesus," I said quietly. I had a lot of ammunition to shoot that one down, but I knew it wouldn't make a difference for him. He was set in his beliefs.

There were some people I knew at work that were anti-gay. Carol, the woman that spread gossip about me, had a heyday with it once she heard, but thank goodness, there weren't many people that listened to her anymore. She'd spew stuff about me, I'd hear about it, and shake my head. I didn't give her the time of day and did not acknowledge her hate for me.

I never understood people like that, but I certainly wasn't going to have a debate with them and how I chose to live my life. My God understood it all, and loved every human being and supported family any way it was made.

The guys were always exactly who they appeared to be. Reserved, fair, smart, loveable, happy-go-lucky men. I didn't know a whole lot about them as people, but I always enjoyed my time around them. Everything was moving right along, and we started planning more when we were together for our next ultrasound. This was the third visit to check on the twins. I was getting bigger fast.

"First things first," Martin said, as he parted his blonde hair to the side after the appointment. "We need to get you some maternity clothes."

"Yeah, let's get some lunch later, too," Ross said.

"Sounds good," I added.

We spent the whole afternoon together, having lunch, shopping at Two Peas In A Pod for maternity clothes, laughing, joking, and both of them loving up on my tummy.

I was grateful for the choice I made to work with Martin and Ross. I felt so special around them. I'm not sure exactly why, except to explain that I felt like the center of attention being that they were both men. I would often daydream about one of them being my partner. 'I want someone just like this for a partner,' I thought.

I knew they were going to be wonderful daddies. I wondered about their relationship. It seemed they got along very well and I felt confident they worked hard to build the relationship they had, that they might have gone through great periods of doubt with one another, just like any relationship.

I thought about Maddie and Ben. In all those years of very difficult times with heart breaking infertility, they'd weathered the storm and stayed together and now had the family they dreamed of.

I thought about other relationships I knew of that seemed successful and happy, and how they worked. I never really knew, of course, because what happens behind closed doors no one knows. But I think a lot of people get a sense when a couple has a good relationship. I had that feeling about Ross and Martin. They were good for each other.

At a vulnerable point in my pregnancy, at about eleven weeks, when I just started to really show, I started to blame Adam for being Adam, for being unable to love me the way I wanted to be loved. I blamed my first husband for cheating on me and breaking his promise to love me forever. I was angry with every man I'd ever been with.

I think it came to a tipping point when a vice president within our company who lived out of state asked me out on a date during one of his visits. He was married, and had rented a red Mustang that he wanted me to take a ride with him in.

'Fat chance,' I thought. I knew he was going to ask me out, and was ready for what I was going to say to him to end it fast.

"So, would you like to go out with me and ride around in the red Mustang convertible and let your hair blow in the wind?" he said. I was sitting down behind my desk, you couldn't quite tell I was pregnant, so I stood up so he could see me.

"I'm pregnant with twins as a surrogate mother, and more importantly, you're married. I've been there done that, Jim, and I'm never going to make that same mistake again," I said.

"It's just for lunch," he said in defense.

He never asked again, and that ended his many visits to our department.

I wasn't that terrible to be around, I'm a relatively happy person, I thought. But was that true? "Pity Party" came to mind.

So, did I think I was truthful? The answer was no. To be truthful would mean that I would have to be held accountable. I thought about all of my flaws and imperfections that I was too ashamed to talk about, or worse, to even think about with myself.

I started to question my own reality. Deception was everywhere. I knew that to dismantle all of the façades would be a lot of hard work. I wasn't sure I was up for the challenge.

I started to deconstruct my relationship with Adam little by little, thinking about it deeply in new ways. What exactly was really there?

I started to get completely emboldened with Adam and asked him questions I never asked him before, such as, "When is the last time you fucked your wife?" He never answered the question directly but would usually say something like, "You know we rarely have intercourse."

I was living this way for years. 'When will I change it?' I wondered to myself.

I became obsessive about his time and wanted to know about his private life and all the hard truths I didn't really want to hear but demanded to know anyway. I was like a slow time bomb. I was acting like a jealous lover, going by his home to see if he was home. Stalking, I believe they call it. I'd imagine a stupid fantasy that I could never prove like coming up with places they went together, things they did together, and looking, seriously looking for things to be mad about.

Honestly, it felt good to ask bold and frank questions of Adam. It was nearing the time I would break up with him again. I couldn't stand myself and how I was feeling about not having a good relationship, or even a real relationship. I didn't want to just break up with him this time, I wanted it to be over, but for some reason I couldn't cut the cord. I finally went to a therapist to help me get myself out of this mess. I remember her saying, "Why don't you just be honest about all of it, Susan?"

Well, I thought that was a dumb idea because I didn't know how to tell the truth. I bent the truth to my own needs, to my own satisfaction. I remembered having the sense of happiness that I was handling it all, telling myself I was like a superwoman or something. I did the denial dramas like a queen.

Ridiculous. Now I saw and felt how ridiculous this all was. My life was pretty fucked up but what gave me comfort was that there was always someone else worse off than myself.

When Hope Becomes Life A Five

The simple fact was that my life was unmanageable. My hormones were all over the place. It was the story of my life. Was I complicating it on purpose? Was I getting pregnant to hide from life, hide from relationships?

I hoped I was being a good mother. I hated it when I doubted my motherhood. I wanted nothing more in the world than to be a good mother. I had my doubts, but I certainly wasn't teaching the boys anything good about relationships. The boys knew nothing about Adam. As far as I was concerned, they never would.

I was living in a state of self-imposed chaos, lying and hiding, keeping secrets. I started to see it all, but simply could not act to change it. I felt so trapped in the whole big mess.

If there was any hope out there, maybe there would be a better life for me.

Things needed to change.

FIFTEEN

LIFE AND DEATH

I got a call from my mother a few days after Christmas. She was recovering from a really bad cold.

"Honey, I still have that damn cold. The cough is persistent, like it has a mind of its own," she said. I had an eerie, terrible feeling about the whole thing.

I called my mom back and said, "Go to Emergency, now, Mom. Call me when you get home." I called my sister, who called my older brother, and then I called my younger brother.

My mom didn't call me back that day. It was so unlike her, but it was late in the evening when she went in so I thought the next day would be fine. I went to work that next day, but she didn't call back then either.

I got a call from the hospital later that evening. A nurse told me my mother had been admitted. She handed the phone to my mom. "I'm fine, honey," she said. "The doctors are running tests (cough, cough cough) to see why this cough won't go away." She coughed through the whole sentence. I heard her cough this way before during a really bad cold in the past.

"Okay, please just let me know, Mom."

I called her again the next day. Still no news. It was another wrenching, long day before I heard from her again.

"It's not good news, honey. I have cancer again. In my lungs." She coughed harder than I've ever heard her cough, and she couldn't stop. She tried to catch her breath then stopped coughing for a brief moment.

I felt my own breath stop for a second waiting to hear her cough again. Nothing. I caught my own breath again just in time to feel my heart drop right out of my body.

I started to hyperventilate. 'It was a death sentence,' I thought. 'The lungs.' I had just turned nineteen weeks pregnant with Ross and Martin's twins.

I remembered that I had signed in our contract that I would not fly after twenty weeks. I called the guys to let them know what happened.

Both Martin and Ross were amazing. "No, Susan. Go." I remember hearing them say in support. I hopped on the next plane up to northern California to be with my mother. I never asked if I could go. I just knew I had to go.

I was shocked. I didn't know anything about lung cancer. I just knew that it wasn't good. Almost five years ago to the day I had helped her beat throat cancer. It was one of the hardest things I'd ever done, taking care of my mother for an entire year. I started preparing myself for the fight. We'd need a lot more knowledge, but I had every intention that we were going to kick cancer's ass again.

During the first cancer diagnosis, she moved in with me for that year and I took care of her when she could barely keep food down, got her to the many appointments for radiation and chemo, and she recovered. It was right before I got pregnant with my second set of twins. I thought, 'okay, so a second round. We're going to have to beat this, too.' I visualized kicking cancer out of her body and obliterating all the cancer cells.

Just as soon as I said that to myself, the doctor came in and looked at me, my brothers and sister, and said, "There is nothing we can do for your mother. The cancer is inoperable and is spreading like wildfire."

I didn't have time to process my mother actively dying. My world was instantly falling apart. That was my prayer the minute I was told my mother was dying. *No. Fuck you, we're fighting this.*

The woman who gave birth to me, the one who loved me no matter what was dying right in front of my own eyes?

'She'll be gone soon,' I heard myself think, then I cried. My grief hit hard due to all the hormones racing through my body. I still refused to believe it. There has to be something. Anything. "What can we do?" I asked. My siblings looked at me with faces of hopelessness and sadness.

We went back into my mother's room and huddled around her. She looked at us, but there was nothing to say. God, what do you say? We didn't know if she's going to make it or not, though the doctor implied the latter. How long will she have to suffer? There were so many questions left unanswered. All we could do was wait. My heart did not want to create a place for this reality within it.

Mom was sitting up in bed perfectly fine, but coughing. A lot. I didn't know if the doctors told her how bad it was or discussed with her whether or not she was going to die, but it sure as hell didn't look like they did. We simply didn't talk about it.

To pass the time, I grabbed the dry erase marker and started playing hangman on the hospital white board. My mom loved crossword puzzles and she used to watch the Wheel of Fortune with my grandmother all the time. No one wanted to play but finally gave in after I gave a few examples on the whiteboard. "Come on, guess a letter," I'd say.

It soon became a contest. It was me and my mom against my older brother and sister. My younger brother had to work that day and wasn't there. She was having fun and I watched her smile and laugh for a few hours while we played. Her coughing never let up, and we finally stopped when she got visibly tired. Her body slumped into the pillows, and she clearly needed some rest.

We left and came back the next day, a Sunday. We were able to be with my mom because it was a weekend. I tried to carry on our hangman game from the night before, but something was different about my mom. She played a little bit, but then was too tired to carry on. The light in her eyes was dwindling.

Before I left to fly home, all of us talked outside of mom's room. My older brother spoke first.

"Mom isn't going to make it," Harold said. I cried harder than I ever felt myself cry.

"I talked with the doctors and they can't do anything," he said. I cried harder. "We need to get all of our kids here by Friday to see their grandmother one last time." I cried so hard my big belly ached. I didn't want to believe it to be true. But it was.

On the flight home that night, I broke down on the airplane when I couldn't get my luggage into the overhead bin. A nice woman saw my big belly and didn't ask questions, just kindly helped me. My mom called me on the phone every night up until Wednesday. I called the nurse to see how she was. She put her on the phone. She could barely talk and was in pain. "I'm here, hon-ey," she said very slowly. It was all she could say.

When we arrived on Friday night, hospice had already been called. 'Hospice is the end,' I thought. I cried more. I could not get a hold of myself and couldn't look at my mom. I certainly couldn't talk to her about her own death. It was happening too fast. The kids had a hard time seeing their grandmother being sick, and as young kids often do, spent most of their time outside the hospital room and out of the hospital every chance they got.

At one moment, I was trying to feed my mom some yogurt. She loved yogurt and when she was staying at our house she would always give our dog Boomer the last bite left in the container. As I spoon-fed my mother, I thought about all the times I held her head up as she got sick during her first fight with cancer. I fed her Ensure then, one can after another. I had held her trembling body and helped her walk again while we fought the fight. I moved her around in bed at a time I could barely breathe, and she started fighting back. Hard. But this time, food wouldn't go down. She couldn't eat. She simply could not eat anything. I was devastated. I looked at my siblings, and we all knew what we couldn't say.

We were losing our mother. To fucking cancer.

I had a long, intimate talk with one of the hospice workers. Her name was Anne. "Death is as close to life as you can get, Susan." I didn't understand. I do now but didn't then.

She asked, "Who taught you about life?"

"My mother," I said crying.

"Now, she is teaching you about death." Anne's short, soft blonde hair cupped down lightly like feathers just below her ears. She had a face you could talk to forever. I'll never forget her gentle voice, her engaging, friendly, loving face guiding me, teaching me about death.

"Her body is breaking down. That's why you don't really see your mother. She's sick and the cancer is breaking her body down, organ by organ, to die. That's how it is with death." She held me close in the hospital hallway on a bench just down the hall from my mom's room.

"With a new life, (she patted my pregnant belly) things grow with health and light, they multiply and generate new cells and organs, growing almost like flowers. A fetus becomes a baby. In death, the cells shrivel, cease to work, and the body dies. The mortal shell, the body, is left and the spirit flies free," she said.

I cried non-stop in her arms.

"Go talk to your mom. Tell her what you're feeling," Anne said.

"Okay, when I stop crying," I said.

"Grief is only grief, it's a feeling. It's okay and won't be this way forever. Don't ever think you need to let go of your mother. Carry her with you always. Let her live inside of you. Carry her with you until it's your time, and your children will do the same for you."

I'll never forget Anne. She gave me such a beautiful gift that day in the hospital. I vowed to pay it forward to others who need to hear the same thing.

I went in to talk to my mom. Just us.

"Don't be sad, honey," she managed to say.

I started to cry again. I put my arms around her and sat next to her on the edge of the bed. She knew, and I did, too, that no words were needed about her imminent death.

I never knew these memories would break my heart open in the wildest and best possible ways. I thought about all the words of 'hope' around her apartment. In the last year she bought everything she could find that had 'hope' on it. She had sent me a gold 'hope' ornament that now hangs on our Christmas tree every year. She made me a pillow that has 'hope' embroidered on the cover. She literally had hope all over her apartment, in wood, metal, yarn and in every different decoration there was. Hope truly was all around her. She'd recently found a little kitten at the place she worked and called her Hope.

She put her hand on my pregnant tummy.

"I can't wait…for your little girl," she said.

"No, Mom. The twins inside my belly are not mine. I'm a surrogate, remember?"

"Yes, yes I do," she struggled to say. She rubbed my belly and I hopped my pregnant body up on her bed to lay with her. I felt bad that the twins had to feel the sadness I was feeling at that moment.

It was unfathomable sadness.

"When you give birth to her, give her the blanket I made, and the little white dress I made for her."

We'd talked about me having a little girl many times, but I'd pretty much given up on having any more kids, and I knew this surrogacy would definitely be my last. Still, I kept the little white dress she made for my little girl in my storage bin in the garage, along with the girly pastel ribbon blanket she made. She used to joke with me that she wanted me to have a little girl exactly like myself. I was fierce and independent as a child, and as an adult, too.

Maybe I was more like her than I ever imagined.

"Mom, that ship sailed. I'm not having any more kids. I'm not even married, remember," I said.

"You will," she said.

My mom was the most maternal woman I'd ever known. She loved to hold and love babies. If there was an infant baby within five feet of her, and if she had time, she'd ask a stranger to hold their baby. Most, if not all, handed their babies right over. She loved babies.

I thought maybe she was thinking way outside the box, or maybe she was a little out of it, but I didn't care. I loved the sweet thought of having another baby of my own, but serious doubt loomed over and I didn't give it another thought, although some part of me wanted to believe it.

I couldn't really comprehend the thought that I would have another child of my own. I was perfectly happy with my boys. Brian was a senior in high school getting ready to embark out on his own, and Steven was a freshman in high school. I was such a proud mom to have two boys who had grown up to be good people.

I didn't argue with my mom about it. I just listened and felt it was rather insignificant with what was going on with her right now. I wanted every moment I could get with her. I wanted her to know how very much I loved her, and that I'd always carry her with me in all I do and all I create.

"Just promise me," she coughed.

"Yes, of course, Mom. I will give her the dress and blanket. I still have it."

We all got ready to leave again after we made arrangements with Anne to put my mother into a convalescent home. I was against it, but we had no other choice. The hospital could not keep her. We all agreed to do this temporarily and would make decisions over the next week and visit her next weekend. I knew my mother would hate the idea of a convalescent home, but she was getting worse by the day, and was almost incoherent by the time we left that late Sunday evening.

Time knew my mother's life was ending. We didn't. And we didn't want to.

"I love you, Mom," I said.

Those words would be the last words I said to her.

I held her hand like I did when I was a very little girl. Her hands. They weren't soft and feminine, they were larger than life, hard-working womanly hands now freckled with age spots that I was sure to get when it was my time. The hands of a woman who has had a tough life, but loved her kids fiercely. I would know her hands anywhere. I see them now, in my mind's eye, all the time. The hands that held my head when I barfed, grabbed a cool washcloth when I needed it on my forehead. That held me when no one else would, that were with me during the embryo reduction, one of the hardest times in my life, holding me and loving me no matter what. Her hands that held me close, and said she wished she could have protected me when I was a little girl, but she wasn't strong enough herself.

"I love you, Susan," she barely whispered back, then coughed loudly, then softly. I can still hear those words, eleven years later, and I'm sure I'll hear them for the rest of my life. I let go of her hand and walked backwards slowly toward the door staring at her hands placed on top of her chest. I had the feeling I'd never see her again, but hoping, hoping, hoping, hoping I would.

It is a moment I will never forget.

After receiving updates on her condition, we planned to meet up again that coming weekend to see what other place might have a bed for her.

On the following Tuesday, I was at work when I had an unbelievable need, an urge to go see her. I was working on a project at the computer and literally got up from my desk and started to walk to the door without my purse, without anything. I just started walking out the door to get home, get a plane ticket, and go see her.

One of my co-workers, Emily, met me at the door. "Where you going Susan? Are you okay?" she asked.

"I need to see my mother," I said. "I feel her. Here, like a whoosh of wind around my shoulder and side. I said, mesmerized.

"Call the center, Susan. Call now," Emily said.

Still in a trance, I called to get an update. The nurse on duty said, "Your younger brother was here to see her earlier." It made my heart smile. She continued. "He held her hand, left the building… and then she passed away. I'm so sorry."

Grief knocked me down like a ton of bricks.

She was gone.

I felt her, she moved around me like a strong, invisible wind after she died. I can still feel that feeling, that whoosh to this day. What I believed to be her spirit danced around me the day she died, and then was gone.

It's hard to remember what happened between the time my mother died and when I gave birth to the twins. Life and death were so close together, and grief was my constant companion.

"You don't have to let go of your mother," Anne said. "Carry her memory inside of you." This gave me a lot of peace. I didn't want to let go of her because she did live inside of me.

My mother lived for exactly seventeen days after she went to Emergency for a cough.

Seventeen days.

The aggressive cancer moved and grew fast like an active mold until it squeezed the air out of her lungs and her heart stopped. I watched the life and light in her hazel eyes wither, and then eventually go out.

My mother died from lung cancer on Tuesday, January 15, 2008.

I miss her desperately.

SIXTEEN

GRIEF-STRICKEN

You never think your own mother is going to die, until she does. I still felt guilty for being so sad while I was carrying the twins, but I couldn't help it. I'd rub my tummy often and talk to them.

"Your life is going to be full of love. You are so wanted with two daddies waiting for you," I'd tell them this often.

Adam left a phone message for me, and I eventually called him back. It occurred to me that I didn't call him when my mother died, and that it was perfectly fine for me to wait. I knew he couldn't be there when I needed him, so I didn't bother.

We continued to see each other, though I started not to look forward to our visits. It was almost as if I didn't even care if he came over or not. It was the same old thing. He'd come over, we'd have sex, and that was it. He'd planned a getaway for us that was coming up soon, and I'd lost interest. I only thought about my mother. As time went on, I thought it might be nice to get away after all.

In our encounters, Adam would stay for some conversation, but it was pretty empty. How much could you really talk about when you've known each other for years but aren't really in each others' lives, haven't grown and learned and shared all of life together. We never went anywhere. We would always just lie around in my bedroom.

I was finding that I preferred spending time alone and was starting to really enjoy my job. I was getting great annual reviews and doing things I never thought I would without a college degree. Kevin was giving me more responsibility. I thought again about finishing my degree, but I had two years left, which felt daunting, and I always let math hold me back.

One time after sex, Adam and I were discussing education. "Finish your degree, Susan, you never know where it will take you," Adam said.

"Yeah, I'm sure I'd get a better position and make more money if I finished my degree, but I just can't find the time with all I have in my life right now. But maybe after surrogacy, when a lot of time will open up," I said, lying on the bed thinking about it.

"Unexpected things always happen with a degree," Adam said, starting to get dressed to leave my house.

"What do you mean? I know a lot of people who I would never guess have a degree, or a higher degree, because they seriously don't know shit," I said.

"Well, that's true, but it's just the fact that you have it that makes the difference, he said.

I knew that to be true. It was a fact in the working world.

"The world doesn't run on love, Susan," Adam added. He looked at me like he'd lost all hope for love.

"It should, we'd be a lot better off."

This reminded me that he believed in the old school system. The old white man patriarchy. The one I grew up in. The one I knew very well and was beginning to rebel against. We simply couldn't be more opposite kinds of people. We definitely wouldn't make it together in the real world, I thought.

I patted my large tummy and thought about college. 'Maybe, one day.' I focused on positive things because I wanted the twins to feel my happiness, my love.

I was always saying "maybe, one day." I was sick of that old song. I realized it was always playing, and that I took a second seat with everything. The one day was feeling closer to now.

The twins were due in April, and it was the middle of March. I got a nasty sinus infection that would not go away. I visited the doctor twice and could not get rid of the infection. It landed me at home to rest while I worked on taking better care of myself.

I went back to my journal to recall those days, and there wasn't anything but incidental appointments written in it. I think back and recall I wasn't feeling anything but grief, numbness. I don't remember a lot of the second half of my pregnancy with the twins. I stopped writing in my journal.

I thought of my mom all the time. I thought of how she would always touch my shoulder lightly and say, "I'm right here, on your shoulder. Always."

I knew this would be my last surrogacy. No more. I knew this for sure.

I began to lose interest in everything I thought I cared about. Adam, surrogacy, and the things in my life that were not working for me any longer. Even though I loved being pregnant, I knew it couldn't go on forever. I was letting go a little at a time, and during those thoughts, I had a quick flashback to when I told my ex-husband our marriage was over. It was a transitional time for me, and a time-altering moment. I knew it was happening again. Things were changing. I was changing.

The guys sent me recordings of themselves on cassettes reading children's books which I would play for their twins. I put the cassette player on my tummy every night for the growing babies so they could hear their daddies' voices reading to them. Boomer, our sweet lab-retriever golden dog would put his little head on part of my very big and growing belly and listen to the guys read. I'd eat ice cream, lots of ice cream. The twins would kick this way and that way, and Boomer would lift his head just slightly, and then put it down again and sigh.

I was bigger this time around probably because of all the time I spent in bed after I got home from my mother's funeral service.

It turned out she had helped countless people from the fabric store she worked, none of which I knew about. She had more friends than I ever imagined. One woman told me that my mom made her veil for her wedding dress. She'd gone to the fabric store my mom worked at in tears thinking she could make one but really didn't know how. My mother offered to make it for her in three days as a gift for her wedding. After people shared their stories about my mother, it was like I had a new part of her to hold. I never knew before. I sobbed during her entire service and had zero energy. I seriously thought my tear ducts might soon dry up forever.

Most of my thoughts during this time were focused on memories of my mother. I'd have reoccurring memories come out of nowhere about her.

One particular time that I played over and over was when I was first out on my own. I must have been twenty-three or so. For a few years I was drinking and doing recreational drugs and it had started wreaking havoc with my life. I knew it, and would eventually quit cold turkey with no help. Looking in the mirror one morning I said to myself, "Who is this woman, and what have you done with Susan?" Before I quit, I called my mom to ask her for money to pay my rent. I was desperate and had no other alternatives. I had a job as a receptionist but spent my money in all the wrong ways.

'Of all things to remember,' I thought. Goddammit. I wanted the happy, better memories with my mom, but couldn't remember them then.

"Mom, I need some money. I hate to call you and ask you this, but it is the first time I've ever asked you for money. Could you send me a few hundred dollars?" I begged. This was back in the early 80s. I held the end of the receiver so hard I thought I'd break it.

"Honey, I don't have it," she said. As much as it hurt, I believed her. What I didn't know then was "No" was one of the best things she could have said. It taught me not to depend on someone else, to dust myself off, and make my own money. Or in this case, manage it better.

I got completely wasted that night and then quit drugs the next day, forever.

That was back in the day when I ate Häagen-Dazs Chocolate Chocolate Chip ice cream for dinner. On some lost days I would go across the street to the local 7-11 and buy a SHAPE magazine, pining away, looking at the women I wanted to look like and be, and would buy a diet soda and a candy bar. I'm not sure I ever ate real food then.

Another time I thought of was when I was in high school and just made the cheerleading squad, after I didn't make it. I hadn't made the squad I wanted so desperately to join and went through all the crying and disappointment over it. A few weeks later, the cheerleading leader called me and another girl to tell us we made the team after all because they wanted seven on the squad instead of five.

I was beyond happy! I wanted that cheerleading position more than anything in my teenager life.

Two weeks later my mother told us were moving. I was devastated and refused to go. I'd just become a cheerleader!

She'd met a bus driver named Mel and wanted to move to Colorado. It's funny how, as a teenager, you never think about your parents' personal life until it affects your own life. My mom wanted to get married, again, to a man she just met! My sister and I were not having it.

My sister was a senior in high school and decided to stay with friends to finish out her senior year. I was a freshman going to be a sophomore. I begged my closest friend to live with her, her single mother, and her younger brother. It was a lot to ask of them, and yet they opened their home to me. I'll be forever grateful to them, and my bestie's mother became my surrogate mother for those trying times in high school.

I knew nothing about life then, though I thought I did. I probably would not have even graduated high school if it weren't for the close friends I had that helped me through, especially Terrie, picking me up and driving me to class when I didn't want to go.

I painfully remembered seeing my mom's excited face, smiling as she looked back at me in the middle of the street as she, her husband-to-be, and my little brother were driving down the street to a new life.

To pass time during my pregnancy, Terrie and I spent a lot of time going shopping for this and that. We always had a good time together even if we were doing absolutely nothing. The boys were busy with school. Brian was rapidly approaching the end of his senior year and planning for college. I still had the nasty sinus infection. It just wouldn't go away and lingered for months.

The guys, Ross and Martin, were as wonderful as anyone could be about my mother dying. They knew my heart was broken. They offered their condolences and sent me a beautiful bouquet of flowers. They were a special kind of friend to me. I simply adored them. They called often to see how I was and came to see me at home whenever they could.

Yet, grief continued to hold me down, and it was not letting go.

I felt really bad the day I saw Dr. Kazman for my once a week check-up while I was getting to the end of the pregnancy. I was sure my head was going to explode from the sinus infection. Dr. Kazman said, "You need to have this looked at by a specialist, Susan." He referred me to his personal ENT doctor.

"Okay, I'll go over now if I can," I said.

"We'll call to see if we can get you in," he said. I heard him clear his throat and say, "I hope you aren't thinking of doing another surrogacy are you?" I looked up at him as I started to get up from the exam table.

"No, I wasn't. No future plans for surrogacy."

"Good. I just wanted to let you know that I won't approve it," he said with a judgmental face. It felt awkward, cold.

"I didn't think you would, Dr. Kazman," I said feeling like my nose and around the nose was going to fall off my face from the infection. "I'd love to know why though."

"Is it the money?" he asked, looking straight at me with an inquisitive face.

"I thought you knew me better than that. I don't need this income. It's nice to have, but I don't need it. I have a great job that pays well, and I love what I do. I happen to love being a surrogate mother. There just aren't a lot of women that do what I do. I have to admit I have felt rather addicted to it, but not as much as I used to," I said, hoping we could have a conversation about it." I moved around uncomfortably on the exam table.

"You'll get along just fine when you enter menopause," he said, backing up on his chair. He put some instruments into the sink to be sanitized. "Hormones will work for you. I'm sure you'll go that route," he said. "You know, bioidenticals." I knew all about bioidenticals, and I hoped I wasn't that close to menopause.

At least he understood the hormone part.

"You have to find something else then, not surrogacy. I'd only approve a pregnancy if it would be for your own child. One more pregnancy," he said.

It was funny to hear "one more" from him! I was usually the one that said that, and I had no plans for one more.

I looked straight into his eyes. "You do think it's the money. Don't worry, a lot of people do. It's not that for me. There is no price you can put on having a child for someone else, and there never will be," I said firmly with confidence. I looked past his shoulder at my clothes on the chair. I was ready to leave.

I would eventually tell him at my last postpartum visit that he was one of the best doctors I've ever had. But I felt that what he said was some cruel scheme to keep a woman from knowing her power, even if it is with pregnancy, with bearing life. Who was the judge here?

The focus of it all seemed to be on what pregnancy did to woman's body and that was perceived as negative, rather than the focus being on what her perfect body just did, bore a child. Despite all my thoughts and feelings on the broader subject, I had thought maybe all the pregnancies were starting to affect my body. I know it was affecting my mind. In any case I knew that part of my life was nearly over. I was forty-eight years old, and thirty-eight weeks pregnant with the twins.

On the way to the ENT's office, I hit bad traffic because it was late afternoon. There must have been an accident somewhere along the way as it was worse than usual. I looked over at the car pool lane and thoughtlessly believed I had more than two people in my car. I put my blinker on to get in the car pool lane. I needed relief, and my sinus pressure was debilitating. I thought I'd better get to the doctor soon or I will have these babies in this lane, by myself.

As soon as I pulled into the car lane, I saw red lights behind me. I pulled over to the side of the road and waited for the officer to approach my window. He came to the driver's window and he peered in at my round, very pregnant belly that barely fit behind the wheel.

"The baby isn't born yet." He said then he looked down and started to write my ticket.

"Twins, they are twins, two babies and I'm on my way to the doctor," I said.

"Well, they need to be in a car-seat to be considered a real person."

I didn't fight it. I was wrong to get into the carpool lane but couldn't help but think if he were pregnant with twins at thirty-eight weeks, they'd be real persons to him, too. He handed me a ticket and made me late for my appointment. Months later after the twins were born, I'd fight the ticket and win.

I started feeling light labor pains that night but wasn't sure because the pain in the front of my face from the sinus infection was worse. The doctor prescribed some heavy-duty antibiotics that made me sick to my stomach. It took everything I had to take them; I had to cut them in half and eat them with food.

It felt like my grief was still holding me down. It would appear out of nowhere. Days, weeks, months were just moving along. I just kept moving forward, when bam, I wouldn't even know what hit me and I was on the floor crying, aching with grief. Sometimes I loved too much, felt too much, and then some days I felt nothing at all.

SEVENTEEN

JOURNEY #5 BIRTH

A few days later after dinner, I felt a trickle of water drip down my legs while I was cleaning up the dishes. It wasn't pee. 'It was time,' I thought. It was an early evening on a Saturday, and Terrie happened to be over at the house having dinner with me. Brian and Steven were planning their weekend.

"I think it's time," I announced. Everyone looked at me with a surprised face but said nothing.

"What?" Terrie finally said. "What?" always seemed to be the response to "it's time" when you were pregnant. No matter how many times I've had a baby that was the most always what came out first.

I called the guys. Ross and Martin toggled back and forth between Los Angeles and New Jersey for work, and they happened to be in Los Angeles because the due date was close. I asked them to meet us over at the hospital for me to get checked. I was pretty sure, but not totally sure, and wanted medical intervention. It was a tiny bit of liquid. I wasn't completely sure I was in labor, I still had the sinus infection, and I wanted to make sure the twins were healthy and okay. They agreed.

Dr. Kazman did a quick exam and said I was going through the same thing I did with the first set of twins. I had a small amniotic leak and eventually the damn would break. He wanted to do an ultrasound to check everything and ordered one, but ended up saying to me, Terrie, and the guys, "Make plans everyone, it's baby time."

The guys arranged to have a private room for us at the biggest hospital in Los Angeles. Right outside the large window and across the street was Bloomingdales, and an advertisement for the television show, Lipstick Jungle. It was the largest and most decorated birth room I've ever been in. I think I liked the privacy most.

The twins were born on a Saturday in March 2008. To say I was happy when I heard their cries as they came into this world is an understatement. I was so happy, and then a bit bittersweet. I was overjoyed for the guys, now a family, and happier to claim my own body again after my third C-section. Ross held my hand during the C-section. Martin wanted to see more of what was happening on the other side of the blue curtain as the babies were coming out of my abdomen.

Little Boy was born first at 7 lbs. 2 oz., and Little Girl born next at 6 lbs. 12 oz. They were thriving, healthy, and beautiful. Their new daddies were enthralled as their babies came into the world.

Their smiles said everything and are embedded in my mind along with the memory of when they first held their children. Ross put the babies up to my cheek to cuddle. I reached out and put my head close. New life made me feel so good. I nuzzled both of the twins and whispered, "Welcome to the world, little ones."

I keep a treasure photo memory box at home for every journey I've taken. Each one has been a different journey and each box has various things in them. This journey box holds many fond memories, pictures, cards, one baby blanket from the hospital, pink and blue bubble gum cigars, one cute little blue bonnet, and one Sony MC-60 microcassette tape of the guys reading books. Also in the box are trinkets the twins made for me when they were toddlers, two little shell bracelets from each, and love notes that read, "Love, Love You." I'll always keep and treasure them all.

Every experience has given me a gift I could never get any other way than being a surrogate mother. The experience of surrogacy is often indescribable; I struggle to find words to express my gratitude and the feelings I will forever keep in my heart.

This was the beginning of two new lives, a family and my own life — it was the end of my surrogate journeys.

I was starting over. Again.

EIGHTEEN

DROWNING

I t happened just like this: I fell in love with a man ten years ago that I couldn't have as a partner because he was already taken. He was a married man. Then, I realized the love I thought existed, or I consciously planted there for a while to fill my needs, really didn't exist at all. It was a fantasy love, a one-way love. It was ruining my chances for any real love that I craved, and wanted for the rest of my life. I had to fall out, by myself, me. I had to fall out of love with this man, and I had no idea how.

Two months after the birth of my third set of twins, Adam took me somewhere I wanted to go. We finally were going somewhere together, to stay overnight: I would actually get to sleep with him. I really needed to get away, and the information Adam sent to me via email about the hotel listed it as "99 steps to the beach."

He had me at "beach." I love the ocean and anything close to the water is fabulous with me. I thought of this place that might cater to us with nice adult drinks while we lounged at the pool, even though Adam doesn't drink. My fantasy button was turned on and I thought about us walking along the beach together, naked toes in the sand.

It was about six months after my mother died, and I was just starting to feel like myself again after the birth of the twins. I was holding on to Adam harder than ever before. I wanted more of him. I wanted him to want me, to want to be with me. I pretended to think I never needed anyone, but my actions proved otherwise.

I'd just gotten back into my regular clothes after a few Weight Watcher meetings. I was a lifetime member and I still am to this day. It has always helped me to have someone weigh me so I couldn't cheat and so I didn't have to own a scale; I hate scales and never wanted one. I did really well getting back into my old work clothes, though I'm sure it was also because I was too cheap to buy new ones. Clipping coupons for life has an impact on your soul to be frugal.

"It will be wonderful," Adam said. I nodded my head to agree when he opened the door for me to slide into his red Mustang and take off for the hotel, which was about twenty-five minutes away. When he made it to the driver's side, he pulled his collared green shirt down over his slightly exposed mid-section just covering his Levi's. Over the years, I noticed his mid-section getting a little larger, pushing his shirts forward as he pulled them down harder.

He got in and we took off for our little get away. His car was a newer version of the vintage sporty style Mustangs. He said that he was teased constantly by friends and parishioners at the church for getting such a car.

"You know, my wife found a long blonde hair on this seat from last time you were in it." What he didn't say was I'd only been in his car one time before, years ago when I was looking at it. When he first bought it. I never rode in it - I just sat in it.

"Really?" I said, with a little "Hmpfh" sound. He pulled another long strand of blonde hair off the seat near my head and he threw it out the window as he was driving. His wife had dark brown hair, but he often drove parishioners to and from events. I doubt many of them had long blonde hair, though.

We made it to the hotel and threw our bags of clothes on to the bed. The hotel was not 99 steps to the beach. It was on a major street with no crosswalk, and we'd have to be seen out in public, which freaked Adam out. Then, if we made it that far, we would have to make our way over tons of large rocks to even make it to the beach. I didn't see Adam doing any of that and we were only staying one night.

I had set myself up for disappointment with my crazy expectations. Everything felt so wrong. Even though I was excited to get away and go with him, I was on edge, and it was the edge of myself, like I was done but wasn't done, excited but not, and left with the feeling of just wanting to go home. I thought, 'I'm here, just make the best of it.'

Months before, I bought a brand-new Victoria Secret outfit knowing Adam would love it. It was a red, lacy bodice one-piece. It had more material than most sexy outfits at the store, and it was just then I realized I bought it more for me than for Adam.

Adam looked at me in my new red lingerie and smiled. "Come here, you lovely woman you."

I didn't feel anything hearing that.

We fucked on the bed within the hour we got there, but I wasn't there. We didn't set a foot outside or near the beach, except to make a quick run over to Wendy's for a burger for dinner. 'Real romantic,' I thought.

He made many comments about the hotel and loving the décor. It was contemporary, clean and white. But I thought they were terribly misleading if not outright lying about it being "99 steps to the beach."

"I'd love to stay on the 3rd floor," he said. "Maybe next time we can?"

"Definitely," I said without thinking. It really surprised me that all of a sudden we were actually making plans for another rendezvous? His kids had flown the nest and were both off to college, so he was more open with his time than he had been. Maybe that was it.

"It is a pretty hotel, but I'm sure it'd be better if we could actually enjoy it and take a long walk on the streets to admire all the beautiful art," I said.

"Yeah," he nodded in agreement, but wasn't going to happen. He didn't want to be seen in public with me.

Still, as we lay on the bed together, I was somewhere else entirely.

He often commented through the night, and even through his snores, "Susan, you okay? You're awfully quiet." I was quiet, and wanted to be at home, alone in my own bed. Making the best of crappy situations were always my specialty.

I thought back to a time when I was six years old and jumped off the high dive at the Elks Club after my mother had looked deep into my eyes and said one inch to my face, "Do not go into the deep end. Do you hear me, Susan Ann?" I nodded like I understood.

But just as soon as my mother put my bathing cap on for the first time since the pool opened that spring, I marched over to the fifteen-foot diving board, walked up the steps, and walked slowly to the end of the wiggly diving board. I jumped without hesitation, without fear.

I remembered it well. I went down, down, down into the water. I let out a little cry for help, and opened my eyes seeing no one around me, just the legs of other kids and people, kicking, and swimming. I flailed my arms to try to reach the bright sunlit top of the pool. It seemed so far away. I pushed off on the concrete with my feet and started to float slowly to the top. Too slowly. I wasn't going fast enough and just floated and stopped midway in the depths of the blue, blue pool. Water was all around me like the safety of my mother's womb.

All of a sudden I felt someone grab my little girl body, and pull it up, up, up to the surface. I cried wondering why it was so hard to breathe. My throat hurt. I couldn't breathe. I've since dreamt about the sound of the water as the lifeguard pulled me up to the surface. "Whoosh…Whooosh." The lifeguard pushed me to my side, and I started coughing. I remembered hurting, but I can't remember where, just all over. I've never in my life seen my mother so mad at me as she was then. My mother screamed, "GodDAMN it, Susan, I told you!!"

I was immediately grounded and afraid I wouldn't be able to swim for the whole day. My sister was elated that I made my mother so furious. She danced in a circle around me saying, "Susan can't swim! Susan can't swim!" And my mother let her taunt me. I remembered feeling the hot concrete beneath my bottom for a very long time. It felt like forever.

My mother would retell that story to me many times as I grew up, of how she made a mad dash running as fast as she could to the lifeguard to save me. My mother was not a runner. Then she said over and over that she watched me go all the way up the ladder thinking I would turn back. But I never did.

I felt like that now, with Adam. But, no one was there to save me. I was drowning at the hotel with him. But I put on the bright side of my personality like I did when I was a little girl, to make sure everybody else in the room was happy, almost like it was my job to make others happy. I told him how fun it was that he cared enough to go someplace that was just ours. That was my survival technique, avoiding conflict, or the truth, and always putting others' ease before my own.

A few months later Adam called me to let me know he was going away for the weekend. It was weird because that was not something he would normally call to tell me. I never knew where he'd be if he didn't contact me. I didn't keep in contact with him that much to care if he was going away for the weekend or not.

"Where you going?" I asked curiously, and purposely because I knew it was out of context to ask anything about his life. He was acting so strange.

"Somewhere where I cannot be contacted."

I raised my eyebrows in surprise. "Um, okay," I said. "Where?"

"A get-together for pastors," he divulged. "You won't be able to contact me."

It haunted me for hours after the phone call. I played it over in my head. Why would he call me with this kind of information, and why would I care? All of a sudden out of absolutely nowhere I thought, 'he's going back to 99 Steps to the Ocean? But with who,' I wondered. I was sure that was it. How? I have no idea except maybe the universe was throwing me crumbs to follow.

I had no information about it. Zero. It was just a feeling that I'd come to know as my beautiful, strong, womanly intuition.

I went with it and had to know.

I called the hotel and got a hold of the front desk. They forwarded me to a room on the third floor. My heart was racing, and this was beyond what I thought I would do.

Who would answer? 'Shit, I'm not sure I can do this,' I thought. I had no idea what I might say.

"Hello?" Adam's voice said. He said it in the way that I once thought was so adorable. This time, his voice sounded content and happy. It was a voice to me that sounded like he did something right in his life, and was so very happy within himself, or finally got laid by someone, maybe even his wife.

"FUCK!" I said loudly into the phone.

Silence. I could hear a woman's voice in the background. Probably asking who was on the line.

"Go ahead, tell her who it is, Adam. Maybe it's time everyone knows," I said feeling like I was about to cry. I was so angry. Tears started rolling as I lie on my bed at home. "Some 'pastors meeting. You fucking liar."

I was devastated. He barely said anything. I said everything.

"I'll call you back in five minutes" he said. The phone went dead.

He called me back immediately and we went around in circles a few times but always came back to the part where my heart was broken for the first time in a long time.

"It is my wife. She wanted to come here to look up and down the streets at all the art, so we stayed here because I have points."

I got so upset that I threatened to come to the hotel and tell his wife everything. I was so damn close to going there. I had to be done but I couldn't hurt another woman the way I was hurt way back when. I could not do that to his wife. She would be devastated. It would ruin her life.

I got in my car with the intention of going there to expose him and end us. I wanted him to hurt like I was hurting. I turned from the freeway onramp south, and instead made the turn to go by his house. It was dark. No lights were on. Her car was in the drive. She wasn't home. She was there, at our hotel, with him.

In some insanely dysfunctional way, I was happy it wasn't someone else, but I didn't know for sure, and for once I did not give a shit. Well, that's a lie. I don't care as I write this, but I did then. It hurt. Bad.

I became the woman scorned. I really did, a seriously angry version of that trope. Then I thought about the stupidity of it. He's cheating on me with his own wife! God, what had I become? It was time to fall out of love with him, and this was my invitation.

I'd finally hit the bottom. I was accepting the call to let go of him, of the idea of what I thought love was.

I cried for what felt like weeks but it was maybe just a few days. I drug myself though the memories of all the times I taught him what pleases a woman, and all the sexual things we did together, only knowing now he was pleasing his wife.

Maybe... I was just his sexual surrogate? GOD! I was so done with myself.

I put on my headphones and turned on my iTunes to drown myself in song like I always did. Music made everything better. Of course the first song to pop up was

"Unbreak My Heart" by Toni Braxton. I listened to it and played it again and again and again. I listened to the many songs of love lost, heartbreak, and all the feelings music brought up for me to feel the moment and drown in the lyrics and sadness of the songs.

I could literally feel myself going through the process of falling out of love with Adam, willing myself out loud at times, "STOP, Susan. Stop, let him go." It didn't work fast. It was a slow process.

Finally, I was starting to feel a new softness within myself, a greater sense of me. Was I starting to love myself? I'd get super happy when I hit a point like that, sensing and feeling that thought, and then I'd fall down and cry for days. Music was my lifesaver. "Break Your Heart" by Bare Naked Ladies was on the top of my play list with well over a hundred plays.

I played it so much that one time when Steven overheard me playing it again, he said to me, "That's a pretty screwed up song, Mom."

"I know, right?" I said.

"Seriously, Mom. Major fucked up."

To which I replied, "It's real life, honey, and it's always better when truth comes out." 'If he only knew,' I thought, but would never bring up my lover to anyone until much later on in my life, and never to my kids.

Adam and I continued to have many unhappy conversations over the months. I threatened him more than once and wanted very much to tell his wife so I could destroy us for good. I felt it would be the only way. I could just leave and never see him again. But I'd done that before and always ended up calling him again. I became strong in my reserve to kill us so I could get out of this drama-filled shitshow. I became this mean, angry woman with him. Our affair had gone on for eleven years too long.

It reminded me of how I acted after I found out about my ex-husband screwing around on me before we got married. Back then I stayed in the relationship because I didn't know any better. I married him anyway and at the time thought my twenty-five year-old self was to blame, that it was my fault for not doing something right. I was still stuck in that same story.

All I was meeting in my life were fucking unavailable men! This time would be different. The bottom was starting to drop out. I vowed to myself, feel what you feel, then let it go.

I gave permission to myself to be right where I was.

"God Dammit! Was there anyone out there that could love me the way I want to be loved? Where is he?" I screamed to the sky.

I thought about all the times I was pregnant and missed it so much. I rubbed my tummy and wanted to be pregnant again. I decided to look more deeply at this than I ever had.

Maybe I became pregnant so many times because being pregnant meant I never had to be alone. Someone, even a sweet baby or two was inside of me, meant I was never alone.

NINETEEN

BABY STEPS

I started to become more involved in dating sites and didn't see Adam anymore. I had a few slip ups but realized I didn't like who I was with him.

I met a man named Bill in February of 2009. I can't remember which dating site we were on when we met, but Bill seemed like a nice enough guy. I started to let other men into my life and tried out relationships again. After two dates we continued to date other people and had developed an open sense of awareness about each other.

After four dates, we slept together. It wasn't fireworks but was nice enough. I found that I kept saying "nice enough" for just about everything Bill and I did together. I was compromising. He was a nice-looking man, in an older type of guy way with gray hair over a part on the side. He was eight years older than I was and dressed nicely. He stood just a little bit taller than me.

"Maybe we can start just seeing each other?" he asked.

'Okay,' I thought, and then realized that meant I couldn't see Adam on the side. I agreed. I wasn't completely over Adam yet, but I was working my way toward it. It was a step in the right direction.

Bill lived about five minutes away from me, from front door to front door. He had his own business with several partners selling electric bikes. We had a lot of the same kinds of likes, such as good wine, good books, and we loved to go outside for any reason at all. We walked in the park, went to the beach a lot, and stopped at little cafés along the way. One weekend he got two electric bikes from his store and we rode all afternoon. We were in the getting to know you phase, were semi-like-minded and enjoyed each other's company.

But there wasn't much of a spark for me. Something was missing. I found myself trying really hard to make this relationship work. It was comfortable. He'd been married for a number of years until his wife asked for a divorce. He apparently fell in love with another woman after his wife, and she left him brokenhearted. Something told me he wasn't done with that relationship yet. Both of us seemed unavailable.

After almost ten months together, I went over to his place on a Friday night. He usually called before the weekend and we always had plans. I hadn't heard from him for a few days, so I decided to go over to his place to surprise him with a bottle of wine. He lived in a little condominium five blocks from the beach. I knocked on his blue condominium door and he opened it. I started to walk in, but he was still holding the door blocking my way.

"Um, I'm not feeling well," he said with a stern face.

"Oh, okay" I said still standing on the welcome mat. I was getting ready to turn around and head home but felt uneasy. Something was off about this, and my past experience told me that maybe he had someone else there with him.

"Are you alone?" I asked, knowing I might be invading his space.

"Yes," he said as a matter of fact standing his ground.

This is where I should have turned away and went home. But something deep down inside did not trust him.

"Really?" I said feeling totally rejected.

"You don't believe me?" he asked. He appeared so incredibly sad.

"No, no I don't," I said nonchalantly.

He hesitated as he let his arm fall so I could come in. I was standing in his living room, not wanting to sit down on the couch. I'd been through this type of thing in the past. I've been cheated on and screwed over and I was not going to go forward if we couldn't trust each other. Why did I want so badly to catch him in a lie?

"What's going on with you? Do you want to talk?" I asked. I stood in the center of his living room. The large tv was blaring, he stood there with his hairy gray chest in his jockey shorts with his tummy hanging over the top strap. Several boxes of cookies, crackers and such were on the tables, the couch and on top of counters. I wondered if he ate them all. *'No way,'* I thought. Sure that someone must be there with him, I looked into the kitchen and saw an unopened bottle of wine with two glasses on the counter. He saw that I noticed.

"No, no I don't want to talk," he said. "I want to be alone."

Then I made the stupidest move of all. I proceeded to search the house. Bad move. I went walking throughout his home, upstairs and down to see if anyone was there with him. There wasn't anyone with him. I felt awful. He was telling the truth.

This move I made was because I didn't trust him. It came from years of coping mechanisms that I developed as a child, to protect myself, and keep me safe. My own vulnerability with the question of whether I was worthy of love and belonging. I questioned this drama I created for no reason other than to continually repeat the same relationship flaws that I had within myself, and used it like armor to protect myself from getting hurt. I blamed others, needed to be right to validate the reason I felt so inadequate. This type of armor kept me safe when I was a little girl but I didn't need it any longer. I needed to accept responsibility for myself, not anyone else.

When I left Bill's home a few minutes later, I realized I felt obsessed in finding him with someone, giving me reason to run. I thought he was seeing someone else if he didn't want to be with me. God forbid he just wanted to be alone.

Then I thought about the possibility that I had major trust issues. I recognized finally that I did. Huge ones. I decided to give the two of us time apart.

He had a business trip to China coming up that week. He called and left me a message. "I'm heading out on the business trip I told you about. I'll give you a call when I get back." I didn't call him back.

This was time for me to figure out what's going on with me. Did I want to see Bill anymore at all? I was embarrassed by my actions at his house. I put it on the back burner and thought about all the men in my life I've dated that were clearly unavailable. In one way or another, they were unavailable.

All the men I dated when I was younger who were on drugs, unavailable. My ex-husband who was on drugs and alcohol, unavailable. Younger men I dated on a whim or who just wanted a one night stand for whatever reason, unavailable. Adam a married man, unavailable. And now Bill, maybe emotionally unavailable? It was easy for me to point my finger at someone else, instead of looking at myself.

At home by myself on a Tuesday evening I started to google a lot of different key words. Unavailable. Men and dating. Unavailable men. How do I find love? I pulled up a lot of articles about unavailability and the psychology of why. I was obsessed with the word – unavailable. With why were people unavailable? And how? I wanted to see what an unavailable man looks like, and what kind of unavailable, and why I kept attracting them.

When Bill got back from China we agreed to take a break with our relationship.

"I'm not feeling myself lately. I have been depressed," he said with hesitation.

"Oh, okay." I said, knowing it was best. I didn't want to be a partner to someone who was sad about his life. I mentioned to him that he might want to look into seeing a doctor and ask to have his testosterone checked. I was serious.

I nodded in agreement while I was talking to him on the phone and wished him well. I felt the presence of rejection, but I was strangely okay with it.

I wondered what was wrong with me. I thought he maybe he met someone new and the possibility of that was pretty high. I took long walks on the beach by myself and thought over and over again about unavailability in relationships.

I decided to take a course for self-development and as part of my performance review promise at work. I'd put it off for months and finally decided to give it a go. It was a woman's self-empowerment workshop, a nine-week course online.

I remembered seeing something at work on the whiteboard during a meeting and I'd memorized it. It read, "You can't go back and change the beginning, but you can start where you are and change the ending." I thought about it every day and night. I lay in bed at night thinking about how I could change my ending.

It was January 2010 and I was ready for something new and desperately needed a lift in my spirit. I signed up for a nine-week course about feminine power. I found it when I Googled one day looking for ways to meet men; I wanted to seek new ways, not old ones. I came upon a book to help me call in "The One." I wanted to call The One in! I figured it couldn't hurt to try. I was aware of the whole power of attraction, but for the first time in my life I was open to try anything. I just didn't know how to do it.

I got very involved in the course and included it as research at work, integrating it into the work I was doing for my boss. The course cost a couple hundred dollars, which work paid for because it was part of the work I was doing for my performance plan. It would prove to be worth it. It coupled in with all I was learning at work, with integral development.

The facilitators of the workshop were also embedded in some of the work I did for Kevin. I recognized some of their names doing work like promoting humanitarians, philanthropy and promoting peace in the world. They were all a large group of integral people who were waking up and doing work along the lines of their own creative spirits supporting one another in way I've never seen before. Each one had their own creative work specialty, and taught it to the world on a global level.

The one I was taking was called Feminine Power, spreading love luminaries and evolutionary sisterhood around women on the edge of evolution. There were so many others like the power of positive thinking, aligning yourself with the evolutionary process, practicing nonviolence, working with our emotions and fears. You name it, there was a course for it. They were talking my talk, and I gravitated toward all they were doing. It all involved moving the world ahead in a positive manner and all of it had one thing in common: nature.

All participants of this online workshop, thousands of women from all over the country, were instructed to create a profile and link into a webpage for ourselves within the website. Everyone had homework materials to pick up each new week, which I called self-work. Then we were to create our identity with a picture, and list one intention and commitment at the top of the profile that we expect to get from taking this course.

It surprised the hell out of me that the course had a major, global audience of over 100,000 women from more than 120 countries. I almost didn't believe it because it was so massive, with all kinds of women from everywhere. Was this real? I didn't feel so alone anymore. It was huge and we were all the same, meaning we had the same womanly concerns about ourselves, and the world around us.

The energy created during the set-up of the online workshop was amazing and very well organized for such a high number of participants. Women were buzzing all around in our smaller group creating their identities within their profiles, and introducing themselves to one another. We had about ten in our own small group. We got to know one another online and worked together on our individual assignments. It seemed we were all working toward a lot of the same things, but ultimately were all looking to increase our feminine power and to make connections.

The course enhanced the promise to help women everywhere feel they are on the edge of evolution, and I definitely wanted to be a part of that. The purpose was to awaken to the power of being able to co-create our lives and shape the collective future. A big job, right? Huge!

They gave us the tools to enhance our self-learning into the future. It was amazing. I took the course for my future development. I did the personal self-work and it benefited my work life as well. I had to finish the class by the end of three months, and I didn't miss a class. They had live replays on live phone calls with over 100,000 women! The energy created during those telecons were off the charts. So many women, all of us connected, and talking about the same things! I looked forward to each week and didn't want it to end.

The curriculum was familiar because I was doing it at work every day. It was different through the course because it was directed for individuals but it applied to the work environment as well. Through the research all of these people, ideas and thoughts started to connect for me. I had no idea if it would work or not, or whether I would "awaken" but I had nothing to lose.

I wanted in.

On the weekly calls, the two women facilitators who led the course tried to steer women away the poor me/victim mentality, which is so prevalent, and to pull them into being a different way. It was so interesting to witness. One of the facilitators, a woman, was trained and licensed psychologist, the other was on her way to get her PhD. There were so many women who were confused in life and looking for more. I was one of them! It was the one commonality we shared: We were all looking to enhance our lives.

On one of the calls I summoned the courage to call in with a question. I finally got through after fifteen minutes of holding and the psychologist said, "Hello Susan. What's your question about meditation?"

"I've been trying meditation and wondered how to think outside my four walls. You know like when I'm meditating inside my bedroom?

I felt stupid for saying it, but what she said in her answer will stay with me always because I wrote it down, and was able to listen to it on the replay again and again

"Susan, dear Susan. Stop thinking small. Give yourself the permission to explore the universe. Bounce outside those four walls, there are no limits to where your mind and heart can travel. Give the world what you came here for. You have bountiful gifts to give. Don't hide your talents. Reveal yourself, open wide like a beautiful flower."

I was in awe. What? I could give myself permission? It was a simple concept, but it was a huge awakening for me. I was in surprise and wonder with what she said. She didn't even know me, and yet she nailed me. "Give myself the permission?" Really?! Once I realized I could do it for myself, I did it immediately. The next time I meditated I jumped out of the four walls and was up with the stars.

I visualized myself opening up like a flower and knew I was taking steps to a new life. I could feel it slowly making its way into my consciousness.

There was no going back to my old life.

This course would change the rest of my life. I always wondered how many of the women that were in my group, as well as the larger community, changed and transformed as much as I did.

Taking off the armor and putting down the weapons I've used in the past meant finding the courage to be vulnerable, and imperfect. Upon hearing that and practicing it, I could immediately feel it. Vulnerability. Just the word made me feel like I didn't want to do it again. It took practice. The courage to be vulnerable was unreal. I could dare myself to live and openly show up as myself because it made me feel stronger. I would use my whole heart and call in what I wanted.

I listened to all of the podcasts, did my self-work, and started learning more and more about myself. I answered the questions honestly. The courses were designed around:

Awakening your feminine power

The power to transform your life

The power to realize your destiny

The power to change the world

Awakening feminine radiance

Creating the future of your life

Create our brightest future

And more!

That was a big agenda. And none of it would happen unless I was open to it. I was so damn open, I'm not sure I could be more open to it. I felt like a massive sponge. I'm not sure I lived up to all of it, because it's life work, but I will say I learned one simple and important thing through all of my studies into integral adult development:

To be responsible for myself.

That's it. Be responsible for yourself. Take self-responsibility for all you've done in the past and accept it as it is. By yourself, just you.

I'm not sure how that I came to that single concept but it was so simple.

All of the things we worry about, fear, etc., are really only thoughts we keep thinking. They are beliefs about ourselves that we play over and over in our heads, and most of it is negative. The beliefs we have about others, beliefs about your own life, and beliefs about anything. Beliefs that I'm alone, I'm bad, I'm wrong, I'm worthless, I'm different, I'm not enough, etc. Then I saw and learned a new concept, "Beliefs are only thoughts you keep thinking." It made such perfect sense to me.

Change the thought, and you change yourself. You simply don't believe that thought any longer. You think things that matter instead. I am enough, I am not alone, I am right. I am worthy. Simple? Yes, but it can be hard to do because you have to rewire your brain and do it over and over again to believe the new things about yourself. And it works!

I read and re-read the book on calling in love. I wanted to use it to find the love of my life. It required time and energy. I wrote affirmations that made sense to me, and started to live my life like my love was already in my life. I moved to one side of my queen bed, to make space for my lover. I made space in my drawer for my love. I even set a place at the table for the man I was going to meet. My kids seriously thought I was losing all my marbles.

"Um, Mom… why is there another place setting? Is someone coming over?" Steven asked.

"Yes," I said

"Who?" Steven asked.

"Someone is coming to dinner," I said. "Not just yet, but someone very special is on their way."

He backed up out of the kitchen and raised his eyebrows. I'm sure he called his brother at college to tell him Mom lost her mind. It made me laugh because I felt like I knew what I was doing. I was putting everything I had into my future world.

One early morning when I was almost through with the feminine power program, just one session left, I woke up about 4:00 a.m. on a work day. But I wasn't awake. I was conscious, but I couldn't move. I literally could not move my body but could move my eyes back and forth, viewing my room at that moment in time. I didn't know what it was other than it was frightening and exciting at the same time. It almost felt like I was in a dream, but I couldn't wake up and I wasn't asleep. I was in a different consciousness, or, was I? I was in reality but I couldn't move my body. I could see through my eyes but my view was fuzzy around the edges. I'd move my eyes back and forth and see everything in my room.

Everything in my room was normal and there was nothing different about it. I could not move my body. I willed myself to move my legs. Nothing. I thought this might be what it felt like to be completely paralyzed. It was an odd feeling. I closed my eyes and slowed my breathing to try and wake up. I stayed with this for what felt like five minutes.

I started to see a witch doctor on the side of my room. Logically I knew there was no witch doctor in my room, but it was dancing up and down like crazy, mask and all. Was it a dream? I watched the witch doctor dance and it did the witch doctor dance all around the right side of my vision. It put the mask in my face to scare me but I wasn't scared. I was more scared that I was awake and couldn't move than I was of the witch doctor. All of a sudden the visual was gone and I was still in my room. I looked from the left side of the room then to the right with my eyes, still unable to move my body.

I slowed my breathing and closed my eyes. Deep breathing started to reanimate my body. I kept breathing s l o w l y. The more I relaxed and took deep breaths, the more I was able to start to move. Finally, I started to move around.

I was awake but I had been awake even when I saw the witch doctor. I was not asleep. *'A hallucination,'* I thought. I was awake already because I didn't just "wake up" as if out of a sound sleep.

I got up from bed excited and wondering about what just happened.

What happened to me?

TWENTY

AWAKENING

Google and I were meeting a lot online. I was seeing Google more than anyone else in my life. That morning as I grabbed my coffee at work I met Kevin in the break room and told him about what happened that morning. We talked a lot about transformation, awakening and everything else along this topic of conversation. He was a great mentor to me and opened doors for me that I never knew were there.

I grabbed my cup and started back to our office with Kevin.

"Maybe what you experienced was a lucid dream, Susan." We got to our office and I plopped down at my desk on the chair and started thinking about it again.

I looked at him perplexed as he stood by my desk. I'd never really heard of it before.

"Look it up," he said. "See if that is close. I've got a meeting in a few hours, but I wanted to talk to you about giving you more responsibilities with your position. You are doing great work. I'll be back in a few hours."

I didn't want to admit that I didn't know what a lucid dream was but was excited about the possibility of new responsibilities.

This was after a conversation we had recently in which Kevin danced around the subject of surrogacy asking me in a roundabout way if I was going to be a surrogate again. He was great about it, really. He knew it was a delicate subject, but he wanted to know if I was going to be out again for maternity leave. It was also true sometimes during my pregnancy I had terrible pregnancy brain which was sometimes a real disability at work. I told him I was done with surrogacy, no more surrogate babies.

It was time for me.

But right now, I was about to find out more about lucid dreams. Off I went to the computer to look up everything about them. After I read the description, I realized that is what I had, a lucid dream.

Wikipedia said this about lucid dreams:

"A lucid dream is a dream during which the dreamer is aware that they are dreaming. During a lucid dream, the dreamer may gain some amount of control over the dream characters, narrative and environment; however, this is not actually necessary for a dream to be described as lucid."

My mind and brain were so open to change and changing that I felt my brain shifted somehow, my mind became more present.

Kevin was fascinated and we talked for hours about the course I was taking and the lucid dream. We talked about his course of training for the managers and then eventually coaching them one by one with the coaches who were hired. There was a lot of work to be done as we were integrating this change at our company. At the same time, I swear my brain chemistry was changing.

After work I headed home to reflect on all that happened. I spent a lot of time alone contemplating it all. I was trying to figure it all out, but there was no figuring it out. Change was happening. I was trying to understand it.

I turned on some music and picked up a little pillow from my bed that my mother had made for me. I plopped down and listened to the music. I was feeling the music on a deep level, and the words vibrated through my mind. I turned the little miniature pillow I was hugging over to the other side. My mother had embroidered HOPE on it. I smiled, then felt like crying. The grief came rushing back.

After my mother died I thought that moving ahead meant letting go of her. I thought being happy meant I could no longer be sad, but suddenly wondered why couldn't I be both happy and sad, and miss her at the same time? I don't have to let go of her completely. I could choose to embrace her and carry her with me always. I'd bring her with me, she would always be inside of me. She was already there.

I looked out the window from my bed and all of a sudden felt a warm glow throughout my body, and my mind thought, *'God is there, too. Inside of me.'*

"What?" I said back to nothingness. To myself.

This I know for sure: God is me, and I am God.

It felt like a Shirley MacLaine moment, a Hollywood actress who claimed she was God and people teased her relentlessly for it. I laughed, feeling really silly and wondered if I was losing it. I jumped up out of bed facing the window, putting my hands to the top of my head. "What?" Where the hell did that realization come from and was it like this all along? This was something I knew for sure, deep inside, that God is me, and I am God. We are one and the same and he's not some made up guy in the sky.

"Why didn't anyone ever tell me this before?" I was giddy with excitement. I kept repeating it over and over again. "I am." This is the meaning of I AM: I am God, and God is me. I am the earth, I am the stars, I am the universe. I am God, and God is me. Whoa!! Everything, simply everything, felt more clear to me.

I could not tell just anyone what happened. It was a huge awakening for me. My days at work involved more study and I kept to myself, avoiding calls and emails from Adam to see me. I felt I needed to keep it to myself so everyone, especially those close to me, wouldn't think I'd lost my mind.

I decided to go visit my sister, Denise, as she was having a party on the weekend. She lived in northern California. I drove up north by myself along the coast. I had lot of time to think so I made a deal with myself. If I didn't find a partner soon, I would marry myself. Seriously, with ring and all I would marry myself. I was starting to love who I was as a person, a human being.

We went out that night to celebrate. I hadn't seen Denise in a while so it was great catching up with her again. My sister and I were a lot alike and a lot different. She was eighteen months older than me and always tried to be the youngest sister. She had shoulder length blonde hair and brown eyes. We didn't get along very well when we were young, but we were making up for it now that we were older.

We got to the bar that Denise and her boyfriend go to often to meet up with friends. We carried on the celebration from her house. The place we went to was called The Eager Beaver. *'Interesting name,'* I thought. We walked in and Denise knew everyone.

"Hey Terry, get a shot (the regular) for my sister here," Denise said to the bartender. She laughed knowing what was coming for her little sister and she knew her sister was a terrible drinking partner. I couldn't drink for the life of me and was a total lightweight.

"Here you go, beautiful little sister," Terry the bartender said, and lined up a tequila popper up on the bar so fast it made my head spin.

"Thanks, bartender." I said and took my first sip. I was talking to so many people, making new friends, and having a great time. After one shot, my head was already swimming.

I got the family gene that said, "Don't drink, it's really not going to be good if you do." Over the years I knew when to slow myself down and what my limits were.

Three shots in, my head was dizzy.

"No more, Denise. A water for me please." Everything about relationships was fuzzy and fading away and didn't seem quite as bad or as confusing as before. Sometimes alcohol felt so good. It was such a great way to escape. But only temporarily.

A young, beautiful woman named Casey who knew my sister sat next to me and we were having a great conversation. She had shoulder length blonde silky hair, red lips, and wispy, light bangs. Her makeup was natural and highlighted her light brown eyes. We laughed and laughed, and for the life of me I can't remember what we talked about.

She leaned over and kissed me. Not just a sweet little kiss. A kiss that would make my stomach fill with butterflies. I trembled all the way down to my toes. This kiss lit up every fiber of my being. Her tongue danced with my own and met a kindred spirit. It felt like they knew each other, or at the very least, were familiar with one another. It was a kiss that would be the best kiss I'd ever had. It must have lasted a very long time because I was very into it. I did not expect that at all, and I would not have thought to kiss her. I was dumbfounded and delighted at the same time.

When I looked up and opened my eyes every single person I saw was staring at us. They had the kind of expression of surprise that I felt. The people beside us, the bartenders, the people around the bar and my very own sister looked in amazement as we kissed. Casey kept kissing me. I could not stop kissing this woman. I'd never kissed a woman before.

Then the thought came to me. Maybe I would be better with a woman than a man. We kissed more, and deeply. It was almost as if I were kissing myself. I wanted more and so did Casey. We definitely had chemistry.

She said, "Wow, that was amazing."

I was lost for words. I nodded with my head buzzing from the liquor. But I was very there in that moment. I was present in her kiss.

My sister came up to the bar and said, "Suuuusannnn-nnn!!!!!! OMG!!"

I said, "Me, too!"

"Let's go in the restroom." Casey said.

I smiled, got up and followed her to the bathroom. Everyone in the bar followed us with their eyes.

She was tall like me, about the same height so when she moved me up against the bathroom wall our bodies fit perfectly. Our jeans rubbed together as we kissed. I felt her hand pull my short sleeved sunflower shirt up and she touched my naked belly. Her hand moved up to my breasts, it felt like a first time. We kissed more and deeply. Random people I didn't know were asking us to come back into the bar and kiss some more. They tried to pull our arms and pull us back into the bar. "Everyone wants to watch you two," I heard.

We weren't into putting on a show so we started to tune them out. We pretended we were the only ones in the bathroom, but people kept coming in. We were touching, feeling gliding all over each other's bodies. I felt the curves of a woman, naked and so gentle, so real. It was such a turn on.

Denise came in looking for me. "Sistah, everyone is looking for you," she said. I could not believe this was happening.

It felt strange and different which meant I wasn't too drunk to remember what I was doing. Casey's sweet kiss and the faces of those who watched us is what stuck out in my mind the most that evening.

"She's been with other women before, Susan," Denise whispered loudly into my ear. "But, she's also a sweet heart."

"Yes," I said. "Clearly."

I didn't make love to Casey that night, but I did in my mind, and we did in our kiss. I was invited back to her place — with her boyfriend. I turned them down because I preferred only her. I didn't want anything to do with her boyfriend.

The next morning my sister said, "God, Susan I can't believe you. Everyone was watching!" I just smiled thinking about my own identity as a woman. I never really thought I might be interested in another women. It surprised me that Casey turned my life around and made me think about my own sexual identity. Could I be a lesbian? Or did I like both sexes? I thought about it sometimes, about women. It was always a turn on.

There we were with labels again. I didn't need to label it, but I knew I could just be what I wanted, and just be.

On the five-hour drive home, I listened to a voice mail Adam had sent to me. Strange how the more I was ignoring him on purpose that he made more attempts to get a hold of me. The rules seemed to be changing. Then I thought to myself, Do I love him anymore? A resounding "NO" flooded my being. I was so happy, doing the happy dance in the seat playing loud music as I drove along the I 5 south singing to myself. I got to experience kissing a woman and my life seemed to open with more possibilities. It was a happy day with no hangover. I had a headache when I woke up but it went away.

I returned Adam's call when I was almost home.

"You sound really happy," he said.

"Yeah, yes I am. Which is exactly why I am not going to see you anymore. I think this is the end of us Adam." I said.

Instead of going in depth about identity and identity gender and what might be good for me, I told him what happened with Casey. He was totally turned on and said, "Wow, I hope we can get Casey to come down here, maybe even a threesome?" he asked.

'In your fucking dreams,' I thought and this was after I told him we were done. I was a little thrown off by his comments after he said that, and I wasn't acting the way I

usually did with him. In the past we would have laughed about it, played it out and I probably would have asked Casey to come to LA to make that threesome happen.

Adam was now someone I used to love, reminding me of someone I used to be. I felt a gap with us and it was widening by the moment.

Later that evening I was thinking about the word unavailable again. It kept popping up. I brushed my teeth and I looked into the mirror while I was brushing and I thought, I'm the one who is unavailable. *It's me!!*

I'm the unavailable one.

It was such a breakthrough and one that had such a simple answer. I'd been reading about bringing clarity into your life, and the article said, in so many words, that when you see something you don't like about someone else, look into the mirror and you will see what you need work on in yourself. Or when you judge someone, look in the mirror and see what it is you don't like about yourself. It proved true every time. It was me!!

I was the unavailable one.

I got pregnant as a surrogate mother to be unavailable for a relationship. I picked the wrong men because I was unavailable. Married man? You couldn't get more unavailable than that! I didn't really want someone because I was making myself unavailable. It may have been subconsciously, because I was not aware of it then. I wasn't ready for a real relationship, so I chose unavailable after unavailable!

For me at midlife, dating was not a crisis. My identity was not a crisis. I was just finally learning how to be me. It all starts when you finally allow yourself to soften into the mysteries of self, and live and ask the questions. For me, the softening came after a long, painful midlife unraveling. It was fueled by years of doing for others, pretending, pleasing and perfecting and losing myself more and more each time. With the questioning came the pure exhaustion of it all.

I put my toothbrush down, cleaned my mouth off and said to the mirror, "So it was you all along?" I smiled.

TWENTY-ONE

HOPE IS LIFE

*"What I know for sure is that speaking
your truth is the most powerful tool we all have."*

— Oprah Winfrey

I t was early February 2010 when Oprah's producer, Tess, called me again. This time it was to invite me to be in O, The Oprah Magazine's 10th Anniversary special for the May 2010 issue. I was shocked they called. I was told that my story had collected a lot of feedback and was one of the "top ten most talked about stories by their readers of the decade." I was quite surprised they called me because our first experience didn't turn out quite so well.

"So, what's it going to be, Susan?" the producer asked.

"Well, I'm in," I said and added, "what kind of feedback did my story receive seven years ago?" I listened, ready for anything really, because I simply had heard it all when it comes to response on the subject of surrogacy. I say that with some level of confidence even though I'm honestly always weary when I say it and ready for anything that might come out of the sky.

"A lot," she said. "Good and not so good."

I imagined 'a lot' to include a lot of what I've heard in the past, both good and bad. A lot of nice and not-so-nice. It was like that with surrogacy, always black or white. No in-between. You either hated it or loved it. It was then I realized that I had to get my story out. I had to tell my own story with everything, not just the bright side, or the dark side, but all of it.

"Like…" I asked.

"People don't understand surrogacy, Susan. You do because you've been there, done that. The general population is just starting to get it. So, of course, you are going to have a lot of good and bad, but it got a lot of attention."

"Exactly," I responded. "I think you mean drama," I said nodding my head in understanding while holding the phone.

"Yeah," she said. "Same-same."

I said yes because I was over the whole issue with the "Womb For Rent" topic. In working on myself I'd finally come to terms with it.

I'd gone through a hell of a lot of work on myself, my own truth. I didn't blame Oprah or anyone else. I wished I had my whole story, I wished I'd written these books back then, but maybe it just wasn't time.

But, this time I was ready. I was strong enough within myself and knew my passion was different from what most people understood. I was ready for good or bad feedback and to tell other people that I have no regrets being a surrogate mother. It is simply one of the most beautiful things I've done in my lifetime, and something that I am extremely proud of. I wouldn't change anything.

There were ups and downs that changed my life. Things I'd have to accept about myself, and things I didn't really want to accept, but learned to. I learned so much. Yes, I was obsessed with pregnancy, close to addicted. I wanted to be pregnant all the time, but that is a whole other issue in and unto itself, and it did relate to feel good hormones, too.

I reflected constantly on why I was a surrogate mother to eight babies for five families, but the simple truth is that there were many complex reasons. An author friend of mine wrote on Mother's Day about struggles we have in life and as mothers sometimes we feel less than, and we have no explanation for the things we do. She wrote, "Sometimes, you become the mother you never had. And in the process, you find the love you missed." I found the love I missed over and over again every time I got pregnant.

Over everything the most important thing I learned from my experience was I could not always change my environment and those around me, but I could change how I interact within it. That was my peace.

Someone I loved once gave me
a box full of darkness.
It took me years to understand
that this too, was a gift.

—Mary Oliver

This poem, written by Mary Oliver, that I put in the front of this book means so much to me. I chose this poem because I lived it. I lived it with Oprah who was a big part of my own personal growth up to this point in my life. Not just once, but several times throughout my life. I didn't love her per say, as this poem reads, but I looked up to her. I respected her as a mentor. In sharing my story with her, at her request with no monetary compensation, which is normally what happens with articles, what she gave me in return was a box full of darkness.

That darkness was within myself. It was up to me to find out what bothered me about "Womb For Rent" and why I was still hiding, acting small, feeling not enough. During those difficult years I learned more about bitterness, loss, and grief than I had ever imagined possible.

The box full of darkness Oprah gave me, I turned into a box full of light and wonder. I kept asking myself why I needed all these "lessons" in life. Why do I keep getting them? And more importantly why do they keep coming? I struggled for years to pull everything about myself together and find out what the meaning was, why was this happening?

Oprah called upon me again. Why? Was this a test to see if I was still listening? I'm sure it wasn't from her directly, but it was certainly through her, her people. And this was something bigger. It was a universal calling for me. Was I listening?

Around the same time, I received an email from a woman I didn't know named Anna. I often received emails from strangers after the story broke and after I put up my website. She said, "I love what you've done for those babies, Susan. You have a gentle, compassionate heart."

Did I? Fuck yeah I did. I always wanted to be compassionate, but I already was. I just wasn't seeing it myself. People out in the world were helping me make the connection to myself. I was listening.

Then, the moment I thought about my part in the reduction when I was carrying the triplet pregnancy which reduced the triplets to twins in utero sixteen years earlier fogged over my memory banks, my soul scars. I thought I was a compassionate and loving person. Where did the good go? The flashback was harsh and rough and made me feel like an awful, a terrible person, and the shame came back full force. It unearthed and set loose feelings like a Pandora's box, making me feel unworthy again.

'No. Stop,' I said to myself. *'You are every bit worthy.'* I'd taken an eraser and erased away parts of myself feeling as though I didn't have the right to be happy, to live, love, and dream.

'Stop,' I said to myself. *'Hold yourself. It's not always going to be perfect.'* I put my arms around myself in a loving

hug and forgave myself for everything. 'It's all going to be okay.' At that time, and even now, the decision to eliminate a life is determined by a world of right and wrong. But the world was not pregnant with triplets faced with an unbelievable nightmare, I was. The world has no place in my decision, and I don't have to answer to anyone. Only to myself. I didn't realize the weight on my shoulders until the freedom came, freedom to be me.

It was the same for being a surrogate mother. Yes, I received compensation but whose business is that of anyone's but mine? I didn't have to defend it like I thought I did. It was a heavy burden to bear.

I became an advocate for pro-choice once I realized that I had permission to use my voice and make my own choices. I spoke up loud and clear as I processed my own personal experience. As the years passed, I took responsibility for my choices, and then and only then, my life started to change. Radically.

I don't look up to anyone anymore. I'm responsible for myself and will probably still be learning about myself for the rest of my life. We're all human and we all make mistakes. It was up to me to figure out why it all bothered me, and why I was hiding. It took years, ten to be exact, to understand the gift born of darkness.

How when hope became life for me, and how giving life as a surrogate mother gave me life.

A gift of darkness from Oprah, that I will forever be grateful for.

A gift that would keep on giving well into meeting the man of my dreams who finally came to dinner at the place I set for him on Thanksgiving, 2010 then married August, 2011. The gift of life again in giving birth to my eleventh child, a daughter that my mother said would come to me, and starting a second family at the ripe age of fifty.

A gift of life for me, braided together with the magic of hope.

ACKNOWLEDGEMENTS

To all eight of my surrogate children. I've carried you all with love. It is because of you that I wrote these two books, soon to be three. I hope by the time you all grow up surrogacy will be a little more well-known and more accepted. You were created with love. I'd love to list your real names, but I won't because someday you may have your own story to tell. Writing this book gave me strength and courage to tell my story. I'm only sorry it took so long to write it. Love to you always.

Mom, thank you for giving me life. I miss you so much. I know you loved me in the best way you knew how. The love you gave me as a little girl sustained me enough to make me who I am today. You always believed in me, even when I didn't believe in myself.

My sons, Brian and Steven, I'm so incredibly proud of who you are as humans, as men in today's world. These journeys wouldn't have happened if you didn't openly share your mom like you did. I love you so very much and thank you beyond belief for being in my life.

My daughter, Nevaeh, I gave birth to you a little later in life than most moms do, but I know you were brought here for a reason. You're daddy's first child, my first daughter, and we're a family together. You've added more love into my life than I ever imagined possible. Love you.

My lover, friend, and husband, Paul, to say thank you seems so small, not enough. You stood by me as I let my secrets out, one by one, and you loved me anyway. I grew more as a person and learned how to be a partner in our marriage with you. I'm grateful to you beyond measure, because without you in my life and supporting me the way you have, this book might never have been written. I know intimate love because of you.

Terrie, my friend for being there with me through thick and thin for so long! I'm so eternally grateful for our long and loving friendship. You mean the world to me. Love you always.

My brothers, my sisters, thank you for being you. I love you all so much.

My extended family and friends, thank you for being in my life. I love you.

Lauren Oujiri, thank you so much for helping me become a better writer. I'm still learning and probably always will be. You have such a compassionate heart and you're always open to crazy timing day or night with our editing process.

Hugh Howey and FB's 20Booksto50, thank you for paving the way for independent (Indie) writers of all genres. I spent many hours on your websites learning the how-to. You were a huge inspiration to me, as a writer, in so many ways.

eharmony, thank you for being the matching device that helped me find Paul, my husband, when I was forty-nine years old. We were both fed up with the online services and it was both of our last dates when we found each other through your site.

My readers, thank you for taking time out of your life to come into my world for a brief time. As a voracious reader myself, it's readers like you who make it happen.

ABOUT THE AUTHOR

Susan Ring lives in Orange County, California with her daughter, Nevaeh and husband, Paul, and with two very interactive cats. Susan's two grown boys, Brian and Steven, reside in Los Angeles, CA.

If you would like to visit Susan, you can check out her new website at www.susanaring.com

Dear Reader,

I hope you enjoyed When Hope Becomes Life.

My second book, whew, I did it!

I'm at work on Book Three, *Full Circle, A Memoir*, will be about my life after surrogacy, finding the love of my life and going full circle to experience infertility myself, and then ultimately giving birth to my daughter in 2013. Upon her birth and what I thought would be a normal C-section the OBGYN makes a fatal mistake, and I bled out on the table and died. Another amazing doctor brought me back to life and reconstructed my obliterated bladder. What we thought was the end was really just the beginning.

I get many requests about the reality of the surrogacy experience because someone seems to always know someone battling infertility. I'm a huge advocate for surrogacy. It always has been, and always will be, very near and dear to my heart.

It is my intention in writing this book that it helps bring surrogacy awareness. I hope it will create more honest communication, and open discussions around the topic of surrogacy. It is life changing for women to express the truth of their power in helping another person have a child.

If you'd like to be alerted when I have a new book available, please sign up for my newsletter at my website: www. susanaring.com or directly through Amazon at my author central page.

One last note, if you have feedback about my book and would like to share, please consider leaving a review at Amazon or Goodreads. It would be wonderful to hear from you.

Thank you and happy reading!
Susan

Printed in Great Britain
by Amazon